# We Are Baptists

# We Are Baptists

## STUDIES FOR ADULTS

## JEFFREY D. JONES

**Judson Press** ■ **Valley Forge**

*We Are Baptists: Studies for Adults*

© 2001 by Judson Press, Valley Forge, PA 19482-0851

The writer wishes to acknowledge the work of Ron Arena for the sessions "The Bible"
and "The Priesthood of Believers."


**Library of Congress Cataloging-in-Publication Data**

Jones, Jeffrey D.
    We are Baptists : studies for adults / Jeffrey D. Jones.
        p.   cm.
    Includes bibliographic references.
    ISBN 0-8170-1343-1 (pbk. : alk. paper)
    1. Baptists—Doctrine—Study and teaching.  I. Title.
    BX6225.J655   2001
    286'.1'0715—dc21                                                    00-055499

Printed in the U.S.A.

06  05  04  03  02  01

10  9  8  7  6  5  4  3  2

# Contents

# Ways to Use This Curriculum

*We Are Baptists* is a flexible curriculum. One way it can be used is for a six-week program to establish a foundational understanding of what it means to be Baptist. For a shorter, focused study, we suggest using the first six lessons: Soul Freedom, Believers' Baptism, The Bible, Priesthood of All Believers, Religious Liberty, and Autonomy of the Local Church. For a more in-depth study, use all fourteen sessions for an entire quarter on what it means to be Baptist. Still other ways to use these materials include:

- Sunday church school
- a church-wide celebration of Baptist heritage, using other volumes in this series for other age levels
- Baptist heritage retreat

However you choose to use these lessons, they are designed for congregations wishing to learn more about Baptist identity and beliefs. Each session addresses a single theme, which is biblically rooted, as a way of helping to define who Baptists are and what they believe and do. It is our hope that leaders and learners will grow in their understanding of our denominations' heritage and the contributions Baptists have made and continue to make in today's world.

Preparing for each session is an important part of the teaching process. Become familiar with the session objectives and outline prior to each lesson. Since you know the students with whom you are working, you can decide how to adapt the material to fit their needs and interests. Less lecture and more involvement in the learning process usually works best. Be creative!

A few sessions require special materials; however, the following materials are needed for each session:

- Bibles
- a copy of the lesson handout for each student
- pens or pencils
- newsprint and markers or chalkboard and chalk

# CHAPTER 1

# Soul Freedom

## Background for the Leader

Soul freedom. To our ears those words may sound odd. Yet they lie at the very heart of what makes us Baptists. Our belief in believer's baptism, in religious liberty, in the priesthood of believers—all the fundamental Baptist emphases—rests on the foundation of soul freedom. Simply put, it is the right and responsibility of each person to stand before God and make decisions about his or her relationship with God. Only when one has done this can the commitment of believer's baptism be made. Thus, religious liberty is essential. And living in this freedom, we become priests to one another.

Rightly understood, soul freedom is not rampant individualism, although it puts great emphasis on the individual. Rather, it is placing oneself in the hands of God, sometimes through the community of faith, sometimes all alone, but always submitting to God's will. The purpose of this session is to explore this somewhat odd, sometimes unfamiliar, but always important foundational principle of our Baptist beliefs.

"Our key is this: To understand the Baptists we must see the principle called 'soul freedom.' By this we mean the deep conviction that every man or woman has both the ability and the necessity to enter into direct saving relationship to God through Christ. Baptists believe that this is a personal relationship needing no outside mediation or formation."[1] These are the words the late seminary and American Baptist Churches in the U.S.A. president Gene Bartlett used to introduce Baptists to those who might not know us very well. If you want to understand us, he seemed to be saying, you need to understand soul freedom. As true as that is, it is also true that many Baptists would be at a loss to describe soul freedom and the way in which it has shaped our life together as denominations.

The word *soul* is particularly difficult. Its meaning today seems limited to the religious aspect of a person. When Baptists first began to talk about soul freedom, however, soul meant much more. They understood it to mean the very core of our being, that central part of us that provides the true essence of who we are as persons. Early Baptists maintained that the core is free—not that it should be free and not that there should be laws guaranteeing its freedom, but that it is free. God created each of us with a free soul. In this freedom individuals develop a relationship with their Creator and discover whom God intended them to be.

Soul freedom isn't license to do anything or be anybody. Rather, it is the freedom to discover and respond to God's call in one's life, the freedom to find and follow God's will and way. Baptists have always recognized that this is something no one can determine for or dictate to another. Bartlett described two implications of soul freedom for Baptists: "Believing in freedom of soul as the essential truth of the Christian life, Baptists historically have moved on two fronts of religious experience.

---

## Biblical Basis
Matthew 16:13–16

## Objectives
By the end of the session participants will be able to:
- define the principle of soul freedom and its importance for Baptists;
- describe how and why soul freedom leads to differences among Baptists on important issues.

## Key Bible Verse
"Who do you say that I am?" (Matthew 16:15).

---

(1) They have resisted anything which seemed to them oppression of freedom of soul. (2) They have insisted on anything which seemed the expression of the freedom."[2] Soul freedom leads us to resist government involvement in religion so that each person is free to pray or not and in any manner he or she chooses. Soul freedom leads us to insist on congregational government so that there is no hierarchy imposing its will or its understanding of God's truth upon others.

Thus, belief in soul freedom explains our lack of reliance on creeds. It explains the diversity that exists within and among Baptist churches and denominations. Its practice in our congregational and denominational life is also what permits the Holy Spirit to work in our midst, to open new possibilities for us, to lead us into new ways of being and doing, into new ways of faithfulness.

Working all of this out in a context of differing values, divergent understandings of God's will, and different interpretations of God's Word is always difficult. There are no set answers.

Even today the attempt to do this creates intense conversations, sometimes even conflict, within Baptist churches and denominations. The principle remains, however. Soul freedom is at the very core of what it means to be a Baptist. It is a heritage we must both celebrate and protect.

## Exploring the Biblical Basis

Jesus knew the end was near. His Galilean ministry of teaching and healing was drawing to a close and he was about to begin his journey to Jerusalem—and death. It was time for decisiveness, both in his own teaching and in what he asked of his disciples. He began gently. "Who do people say that I am?" He undoubtedly knew the answer, for he had heard the gossip: "He's a prophet come back to life—maybe John the Baptist, or Elijah, or Jeremiah." The disciples reported accurately. It was what they had heard too. All this was safe enough. It's always easy to talk about what others think, what others believe. But then Jesus pushed them. "Who do *you* say that I am?" he asked. Now he had gotten personal. Jesus was asking for an "I statement."

Jesus knew that all the teaching, healing, and casting out of demons he had done was worthless unless they understood that it was more than God-talk, more than making people healthy, more than battles over rules and regulations of the faith. They needed to understand that Jesus was the Messiah, the one for whom they had been waiting, and that God was intervening in human history to offer people new life in God's kingdom.

Jesus couldn't force this truth on his disciples; they had to get it on their own. Confessing him to be the Christ must be their decision, made in full freedom, for that was the only way it would really be their faith—a faith they would commit themselves to, even to death. That was the only way. It still is.

The Gospel writers didn't know the term *soul freedom,* but they wrote about it. Despite ridicule and rejection, the woman came to Jesus to pour perfume on him and wash his feet with her hair. That is soul freedom. The rich young man turned away because he wasn't willing to do what was needed to follow Jesus. That, too, is soul freedom.

Biblical examples of soul freedom go all the way back to the first chapter of Genesis when human beings were created in God's image. It is the freedom abused in the eating of the fruit. It is the freedom lived out in the faithful obedience of Abraham and Sarah, in the suffering of Jeremiah. Each one in full freedom, freedom granted by God, stood before God and decided. Each one in full freedom said yes or no to the call of God in his or her life. That is what soul freedom is all about.

Soul freedom was at work in Peter too. Jesus asked Peter, "Who do you say that I am?" In full freedom, from the depth of his being, with his very soul, Peter replied, "You are the Messiah, the Son of the living God." Praise be to God!

## As you prepare for this lesson:
**Pray for each participant by name.**
This session is about soul freedom. Use that perspective as you think about and pray for the members of your class as you prepare. In what ways do they experience freedom in their lives? In what ways do they struggle to be free? How might the freedom they know in Christ have a positive impact on their lives? Pray that this session's focus on soul freedom will awaken in them a greater awareness of their own freedom to stand before God and make decisions about their relationship with Christ.

**Read and reflect on the Bible passage** (Matthew 16:13–16).

The Bible passage for this session is a familiar one. As you read it put yourself in Peter's place. Who do people you know say that Jesus is? Think below the surface so that you consider what they are really saying, not just the words they speak. Then consider your own reply to Jesus' question, "Who do *you* say that I am?" Again, move beyond the words of your response to the way you live. As you do this, you become more fully aware not only of the great freedom we have in our relationship with God, but also of the great responsibility.

## Beginning

**1.** *Share experiences of freedom.* (5 minutes)

■ Welcome the class members and tell them that the focus of this session is freedom.

■ Invite class members to share experiences in their lives in which they had a sense of being free. Allow several minutes for this sharing.

■ Ask: "Was there a responsibility that went with the freedom you experienced in these times?"

■ Allow time for responses. It may be that it will be difficult for class members to describe the responsibility of their freedom. That is okay.

■ Ask: "In what way(s) was God involved in the freedom you experienced in these times?"

■ Again, allow time for responses. Don't be concerned at this point if class members find it difficult to describe God's involvement.

■ Conclude this step by explaining that the freedom you will be talking about in this session is a special kind of freedom, called soul freedom. Write these words on newsprint or the chalkboard.

■ Explain to the class that responsibility and God are both important elements of this kind of freedom.

## Exploring

**2.** *Introduce soul freedom.* (5–10 minutes)

■ Distribute handout #1 and ask class members to look at the section entitled "Soul Freedom."

■ Ask for a volunteer to read it aloud to the class.

■ After the person has completed reading the section, ask whether there are any questions about the meaning of soul freedom. Material in "Background for the Leader" may be helpful in answering questions or in providing additional information that you believe is important.

■ Next, call attention to the second sentence in the second paragraph of handout #1, which describes soul freedom as both a right and a responsibility.

■ Ask class members to list what they believe are some of the responsibilities that go with this freedom. (Items they might mention are the responsibility to develop our relationship with God, to work to discover and fulfill God's intentions for us, and to take our faith seriously.)

**3.** *Explore the Bible passage.* (10–15 minutes)

■ Explain to the class that although the phrase *soul freedom* never appears in the Bible, it is central to the biblical understanding of the way God works in people's lives.

■ Ask class members to turn to Matthew 16:13–16.

■ Have someone read this passage as others follow along.

■ Ask, "In what way do you think this passage illustrates the principle

of soul freedom?" The material in "Exploring the Biblical Basis" will help in answering this question.

■ After ideas have been shared, ask if anyone can think of other illustrations of soul freedom in the Bible.

■ Explore these with class members, asking them to explain why they believe the items they mentioned illustrate the principle of soul freedom.

■ If class members are not able to think of any illustrations, use the listing of Bible stories that assume or imply the concept of soul freedom in the "Soul Freedom in the Bible" section of the handout to prompt discussion.

■ If class members have named several illustrations, point out the ones that match the listing on the handout. Invite them to look up any remaining references and discuss them.

**4.** *Explore implications of soul freedom for important Baptist emphases.* (10 minutes)

■ Ask class members to turn to "The Basic Baptist Principle" on the handout.

■ Introduce this step by explaining that soul freedom is sometimes referred to as the most basic Baptist principle because belief in it leads to many other important emphases.

■ Divide the class into four groups.

■ Assign one of the four emphases described in this section to each of the groups.

■ Ask the group members to discuss the relationship of the emphasis to soul freedom.

■ Allow several minutes for the group work. Then bring the class back together and ask each group to report. Information from "Background for the Leader" will be helpful in this discussion.

## Responding

**5.** *Discuss contemporary issues related to soul freedom. (10–15 minutes)*

■ Use words such as these to introduce this step: "Soul freedom is not just about traditional principles; it touches on important contemporary issues as well. In the midst of this freedom there are different understandings of God's will and the meaning of God's Word. Part of the challenge of being a Baptist is living with the tension of deeply held convictions and the realization that others, in their freedom to stand before God, have different perspectives and beliefs. Belief in soul freedom compels us to find a way through what can be, at times, very difficult situations."

■ Ask class members to turn to "Soul Freedom and Contemporary Issues" on handout #1.

■ Ask someone to read the first paragraph, which describes the tension that existed among Baptists over slavery in the early 1800s.

■ Ask if anyone can think of issues today around which there are similar differences of opinion.

■ If no issues are mentioned, you could suggest abortion, homosexuality, or capital punishment as possible issues. There are strong and differing opinions on these issues among Baptists.

■ Explore the differing opinions with class members; however, don't get into a debate about the issues themselves.

■ Ask class members to reflect upon the insights our belief in soul freedom might bring to the way in which we deal with such strong differences of belief.

■ Point out how difficult it is to balance deep convictions about

issues of faith with openness to differing convictions.

■ Remind the class that this has always been the challenge of freedom and that it is something for which there are no simple answers.

**6.** *Close with prayer. (5 minutes)*

■ Ask class members to share their completions to the following sentences:

— Today I learned that soul freedom . . . .

— For me soul freedom means . . . .

■ Close the class session with a prayer. Thank God for the freedom we are all given in creation, and ask for the insight and courage to continue to be advocates of soul freedom.

## Notes

1. Gene Bartlett, *These Are the Baptists* (Royal Oak, Mich.: Cathedral Publishers, 1972), 2.

2. Ibid.

# CHAPTER 2

# Believers' Baptism

## Background for the Leader

In a very real sense, baptism is what makes Baptists Baptist. At least it is the characteristic about us that people first noticed and by which we got our name. We baptize in a different way and at a different time than many other Christian groups do. We baptize people when they are old enough to understand what following Jesus Christ means and when they make such a commitment. When Baptists baptize, instead of sprinkling, they immerse the person in water.

As with our other beliefs, there is strong biblical support for the way Baptists baptize. The Greek word that in the New Testament is translated "baptize" means literally "to dip under." This form of baptism is grounded in the New Testament. The time of baptism is as well. Jesus was baptized as an adult. All the New Testament stories of baptism are of people who were old enough to have experienced the saving grace of Jesus Christ in their lives, and they had made a conscious decision to accept Christ as their Lord and Savior.

We can clearly affirm a strong Baptist tradition regarding baptism. Baptism is for those who have experienced the saving power of Jesus Christ in their lives. Because their lives have been transformed by Christ, baptism is for those who are willing to commit to following in the way of Christ. This is what Baptists have affirmed since the day in 1609 when John Smyth baptized himself and a small band of believers in Holland and formed the first Baptist church.

*Baptists believe in the baptism of believers.* A person must be able to make a conscious decision that is based in his or her belief about Christ before asking to be baptized. Conscious commitment to Christ as Lord and Savior requires the asking and answering of important questions related to life and faith. When the individuals affirm that the answers of the gospel are the answers that will shape their lives, they may be baptized. All of this assumes a maturity that enables an individual to make both decisions and commitments.

*Baptists affirm baptism as a human response to God's action.* God has acted in Jesus Christ to save us. That action is an invitation to us—an invitation to faith in God, who with great love, makes the sacrifice that brings salvation to us. Baptism is our response to that invitation. God offers us forgiveness of sins; baptism is the sign that we have accepted that offer. God gives the gift of new life in Jesus Christ; baptism is the sign that we have accepted that gift. God calls us to live lives worthy of the gift we have been given; baptism is the sign that we have accepted that call.

*Baptists practice baptism by immersion.* The literal meaning of baptize, "to dip under" or "to submerge," coupled with strong biblical support, upholds the Baptist practice of immersion. Baptism by immersion symbolizes the dying to the old life and rising again to new life in Christ. This reflects the experience of those who seek baptism and further supports the practice of immersion.

---

### Biblical Basis
Acts 8:26–40

### Objectives
By the end of the session participants will be able to:
- explain why Baptists practice believers' baptism by immersion;
- identify ways in which they have grown and are growing in their own understanding of their baptismal vows.

### Key Bible Verse
"What is to prevent me from being baptized?" (Acts 8:36).

---

**5**

## Exploring the Biblical Basis

The eunuch was an official in the Ethiopian court in charge of the queen's finances. In the heat of the day, he traveled a wilderness road on his way home. He was a religious man, or at least, a man with religious sensitivity. He had been in Jerusalem for worship. He was possibly a convert to Judaism or a God-fearer, someone who read the Law and participated in religious ceremonies but had not been circumcised. As he read the Scripture, he may have asked: How does this religion fit together? What difference will it make for my life? Is this something I can commit to?

In this story, the eunuch is trying to understand a bit more about faith. He seeks answers for himself and his life. Perhaps that would have been all, but God intervened. An angel of the Lord appeared to Philip and commanded him to go to this road, to meet this Ethiopian, to answer his questions, to lead him further along in his journey of faith, and to baptize him in the name of Jesus.

This story comes at an interesting point in the Book of Acts. Persecution in Jerusalem caused believers to escape to the countryside. Philip went to Samaria. There he shared the Good News and baptized the Samaritans who came to believe in Jesus Christ. The story of the traveling Ethiopian immediately follows this story. In chapter 10, the story of the baptism of a Gentile named Cornelius is told. In bold fashion Acts tells the story of the spread of the gospel to increasingly different people. It describes the power of the gospel to touch and transform people in unexpected ways.

Baptism is the focus of all these experiences. Baptism confirms our faith in Jesus Christ and publicly declares our commitment to follow a new life. From the earliest days of the church, baptism has played that role in the lives of believers.

## As you prepare for this lesson:

**Pray for each participant by name.** This session will have the most meaning for your participants if it is directly related to their individual needs and interests. As you prepare, keep them in your prayers, remembering them and their needs and asking for God's presence with them. Be particularly sensitive to those who may not yet have been baptized or who have children who are considering baptism.

**Read and reflect on the Bible passage** (Acts 8:26–40). Read the account of Philip's baptism of the Ethiopian. As you do so, place yourself in the role of the Ethiopian, imagining the questions and concerns that he has as he contemplates the meaning of faith for his life. Then, place yourself in the role of Philip. Consider the ways you can most effectively respond to someone who has questions about faith and the meaning of baptism. Also review the additional passages that are included in Step 4 of the session plan. You may want to look up these passages, so that you can read the context in which they occur.

**Select an appropriate hymn or praise song to use with the class as a closing.** Several hymns are suggested in Step 6.

## Beginning

**1.** *Share personal baptism stories. (5 minutes)*

- Open by explaining that you will be exploring the Baptist emphasis of believers' baptism by immersion.
- Explain that you would like to begin this sharing on a more personal note. Invite class members to share experiences of their own baptism: When did it happen? What led them to their decision? What meaning did it have for them? If there are class members from other traditions, invite them to share about their experiences of confirmation or other conscious, public decisions to follow Christ.
- Thank those who shared, and remind the class that the true meaning of baptism comes in the personal way in which it touches our lives with the power of God's love.
- Explain that our reason for studying Baptist teachings about baptism is to enable ourselves and others in our faith community to experience the power of God's love more fully in our lives.

## Exploring

**2.** *Read and reflect on the passage. (10–15 minutes)*

- Ask the class members to open to Acts 8:26–40.
- Point out that this is one of the early stories of a baptism that appears in Acts.
- Explain that in spite of the Ethiopian's important status—he was an official in the royal court, a man of power and understanding—he was still struggling to understand the word of God.
- Tell the class that this is the second of three baptism stories that appear very closely together in Acts, each one describing the spread of the gospel a bit further beyond Israel. (The three baptisms are

those of the Samaritans, the Ethiopian, and a Gentile.)
■ Present other information from "Exploring the Biblical Basis" that you think will be helpful for the class in understanding this story.
■ Ask for a volunteer to read the passage.
■ To begin discussion, ask class members what strikes them about this passage. Does something in particular impress them? Is there something they don't understand? Does anything seem strange? What do they think can be learned from this story?
■ Ask class members to focus their attention on the Ethiopian.
■ Ask: "What can we learn from him about baptism?" If possible, list answers on newsprint or the chalkboard so that they can be referred to later in the session. Possible answers include: *It comes as a response to learning and deciding about God's Word, specifically about who Jesus Christ is. It should be for those who have consciously decided to make a faith commitment.*
■ Ask class members to focus on Philip and his role in this story.
■ Tell the class that many have suggested that Philip can be used as one model for the church's role in leading people to decide to accept Christ as Lord and Savior and be baptized. Ask: "If this is so, what can we learn from Philip about our role as a church?" Again, if possible write answers on newsprint or the chalkboard. Possible answers include: *We are to be available to help people understand God's word and who Jesus Christ is. We are to play a nurturing role in helping them learn. We need to be responsive to God's leading to be in the places we need to be.*

**3.** *Consider Baptist beliefs about baptism. (5–10 minutes)*
■ Distribute handout #2.
■ Note that "The Beginnings of Believers' Baptism" won't be used in class, but provides the story of the beginnings of Baptists that class members may want to read later.
■ Ask participants to look at the beliefs about baptism that are listed under "Basic Baptist Beliefs about Baptism."
■ Ask them to consider the ways in which the Bible passage you have just read supports these beliefs.
■ Have class members share their thoughts, encouraging them to make notes in the space provided under each statement. Information from "Background for the Leader" can be used to help the class make connections between this passage and Baptist beliefs.

**4.** *Explore other New Testament insights. (10–15 minutes)*
■ Explain that stories about baptism are not the only way the New Testament describes this important ritual of our faith: important references to baptism are made in the teaching of the gospels, the speeches of Acts, and the letters of Paul.
■ Ask class members to turn to "Other New Testament Affirmations about Baptism" on the handout.
■ Divide the class into groups and ask each group to read and discuss one of the passages and then write a brief statement of its meaning for us today.
■ When they have finished their work, ask the groups to share their statements. Write them on newsprint or the chalkboard under the heading "New Testament Affirmations about Baptism."

# Responding

**5.** *Personal affirmations about baptism. (10 minutes)*
■ Ask class members to do some personal work related to this discussion about baptism.
■ Encourage them to look over the notes they took and the lists you recorded. Then ask them to use the questions in the handout to reflect on the meaning of this discussion for them personally.
■ Suggest that they may want to share some of their answers with one or two others in the class. Or, after allowing time for personal work, bring the class back together for sharing.
■ Point out that they began the session with personal sharing about their own baptisms and have ended it with personal sharing about the meaning of those baptisms.
■ Emphasize that such personal meaning is the most important element of this session. While it is important to know what Baptists believe and why we believe it, what matters most is the way in which these beliefs touch our lives and enable us to grow in our relationships with Christ.

**6.** *Close with a song and prayer. (5 minutes)*
■ Invite the class to sing a familiar hymn about baptism and the decision to follow Christ. Possible hymns include: "I Have Decided to Follow Jesus," "O Master, Let Me Walk with Thee," "Take My Life and Let It Be Consecrated."
■ Close with a prayer giving thanks to God for the gift of new life in Christ and for baptism, through which we can affirm our acceptance of that gift.

# CHAPTER 3

# The Bible

## Background for the Leader

You've likely heard the old adage that when two or more Baptists are gathered, there are sure to be three or more opinions. Baptists are a fiercely individualistic lot, delightfully diverse. We've long insisted that there is no mediator between us and God except Christ, that no pastor or denominational executive can speak for us on matters of faith. Our Baptist forebears struggled to secure the right of all individuals, guided by the Holy Spirit, to make up their own minds about what they believe.

What draws Baptists together in all these affirmations is our belief that the Bible is the divinely inspired Word of God—a trustworthy, authoritative source for Christian living. Historian Robert G. Torbert wrote about this commitment to the Scriptures in his book *A History of the Baptists:* "It may be observed that Baptists, to a greater degree than any other group, have strengthened the protest of evangelical Protestantism against traditionalism. This they have done by their constant witness to the supremacy of the Scriptures as the all-sufficient and sole norm for faith and practice in the Christian life. All through the history of the Christ-

ian church, there have been minority groups who have sought to restrict the basis for church doctrine and polity to biblical teaching. Accordingly, such spiritual forebears of Baptists as Peter Waldo, John Wycliffe, and John Huss challenged the extra-biblical practices of celebrating the sacrifice of the mass for the dead, of granting indulgences for sins yet to be committed, of encouraging sacred pilgrimages, worship of the saints, and an excessive emphasis upon ritualism. For their pains, they were persecuted severely by a church which accepted the principle that tradition occupies a position of equal authority with the Scriptures."[1]

Today, Baptists throughout North America and the world continue the witness of those early Baptists. Their goal: to be faithful and obedient to God's Word.

## Exploring the Biblical Basis

The apostle Paul was facing his most trying hour. He was in Rome, convicted of a crime he had not committed, waiting to be executed. The work to which he had given his life was being overcome by persecution and defections. In spite of these afflictions, Paul showed no regret

for the choices he had made. He remained faithful to Christ, fully confident that his death would lead him back to his Savior.

This is the context for Paul's second letter to Timothy. Paul's work as a missionary is over, and his life is coming to an end. It is doubtful that he will see Timothy again—and he may not have another chance to write. So in four stirring chapters he offers urgent advice as a veteran missionary to a younger

## Biblical Basis
2 Timothy 3:14–17

## Objectives
By the end of the session, participants will be able to:
■ identify the Bible as the divinely inspired Word of God, guiding Baptist thought and practice for nearly four centuries;
■ state their personal beliefs about the Bible and their reasons for remaining faithful to God's Word.

## Key Bible Verse
"All Scripture is inspired by God and is useful for teaching the truth, rebuking error, correcting faults, and giving instruction for right living" (2 Timothy 3:16, TEV).

colleague and friend. The message: Carry on. Keep the faith. Be a steadfast soldier for Christ even if that means personal suffering and persecution.

Paul also encourages Timothy to maintain his trust in God's Word. The Scriptures, Paul believes, are the sole antidote to a timid faith and corruption within the church. Paul had seen how leaders of his day had cast God's Word aside, dismissing it as a patchwork of Hebrew thought. He knew that "all scripture is inspired by God" (3:16) and that God's Word is "able to instruct you for salvation through faith in Christ Jesus" (3:15). These were powerful words written in the first century—words that are just as timely today for those who follow Christ.

## As you prepare for this lesson:

**Pray for each participant by name.** Ask that God will use you to plant a seed in the lives of the students, one that will someday bear much fruit and nurture within them a deep appreciation of, and commitment to, God's Word.

**Read and reflect on the Bible passage** (2 Timothy 3:14–17). Think about how you can help your students discover the importance of the Bible in their lives and ask God to make it so.

**Select a hymn or choral praise song to use with the class as part of the closing.** Suggested hymns are listed in Step 6.

## Special Materials

■ Recent newspapers and news magazines

## Beginning

**1.** *Introduce the theme. (5 minutes)*
■ Welcome the class, and then begin slowly reading each item below, pausing between each sentence:

— It is a unique book, deemed by many as our most precious heritage.

— It is the all-time best seller, with more than 2 billion copies sold.

— Parts of it have been translated into more than 1,300 languages.

— More than forty authors over a period of nearly one thousand years collaborated to write the sixty-six books and 1,189 chapters that comprise it.

— It is a splendid collection of people stories, poetry, songs, letters, laws, parables, lists of virtues, direct messages or prophecies, and more.

— It has been a wondrous inspiration of ideas, theories, debates, philosophy, and theology—more so than any other book or collection of books.

— It is, of course, the Holy Bible.

■ Announce that the theme of this session is the Bible and the important role Scripture plays in Baptist life.

■ Explain that we are Baptists today because of the conviction of our spiritual forebears, whose study of God's Word convinced them to break off from the established church in England in the early seventeenth century.

**2.** *Discuss faithfulness and obedience. (10 minutes)*
■ Distribute handout #3 and ask the class to look at "A People of the Book."

■ Invite a volunteer to read the material out loud.

■ Lead the class in a brief discussion of the questions in the handout.

## Exploring

**3.** *Read and examine the Scripture. (10–15 minutes)*
■ Direct the class to turn to 2 Timothy 3:14–17.

■ Provide appropriate background material from the section titled "Exploring the Biblical Basis."

■ Ask participants to read the Scripture passage aloud, using two or three different versions.

■ After the text has been read, list these headings on newsprint or a chalkboard:

— Teaching the Truth
— Rebuking Error
— Correcting Faults
— Giving Instruction for Right Living

■ Distribute copies of recent newspapers and news magazines.

■ Invite the class to browse through the papers and magazines, identifying examples of falsehoods, errors, faults, and improper living. Record the examples on the newsprint or chalkboard.

■ Ask the class members to suggest other examples not found in their search.

■ Review the completed list, and ask the class to suggest how the Key Bible Verse, 2 Timothy 3:16, applies to life today.

**4.** *What do you believe? (10 minutes)*
■ Direct class members to "What Do You Believe about the Bible?" on the handout.

■ Review the directions for this activity and give the participants a few minutes to mark their places on each continuum.

■ When they are finished, ask the participants to compare where they placed themselves on the continuum for each statement. Is there a uniformity in their responses? Do beliefs differ widely?

■ Discuss common responses and differences. Be sure to remind participants that these answers are opinions to be considered, not verifiable facts.

■ Ask a class member to read aloud the words of biblical scholar Henry H. Halley in "The Bible as God's Word."

■ Discuss the two questions that follow the quotation on the handout.

■ Finally, ask the class to consider this question: What conclusions can you draw from this activity and from Halley's insights?

## Responding

**5.** *Write a letter. (5–10 minutes)*
■ Use words such as these to introduce this step to the class: "Paul loved to write letters to his friends and colleagues. His writing was so faith-filled and beautiful that thirteen of his letters are part of the New Testament. In Paul's second letter to Timothy, he urged his friend to remain obedient to God and faithful to God's Word. Now it's your turn to write."

■ Encourage the participants to think of one person—a family member, friend, or coworker—whom they would like to tell about God's message in the Bible.

■ Then ask them to write a thoughtful letter—just as Paul did with Timothy—encouraging that person to be faithful to God's Word. Let the participants know that the letters will not be shared with the class, so they may be as personal and persuasive as they like, perhaps even providing their own testimony about how the Bible has helped them in their lives.

■ When they are finished writing, suggest that they take time to reread the letter, imagining that they have just received it in the mail from a friend. Ask them to consider what affect the letter would have on them?

■ Suggest also that the participants consider mailing their letters if they are comfortable doing so.

**6.** *Closing prayer. (5 minutes)*
■ If your class enjoys singing, close by singing together a favorite celebration song or hymn. You may choose instead to read the words to a song or hymn. Those that relate to the theme include "I Would Be True," "May the Mind of Christ," "My Savior," "More about Jesus," "Renew Thy Church, Her Ministries Restore," "Take Time to Be Holy," "The Vision of a Dying World," "In My Life, Be Glorified."

■ After the song, form a circle and close by giving thanks for God's Word and for your time together today.

## Note
1. Robert G. Torbert, *A History of the Baptists* (Valley Forge, Pa.: Judson Press, 1973), 513.

# CHAPTER 4

# Priesthood of All Believers

## Background for the Leader

The "priesthood of all believers" is one of *the* foundational Baptist principles. Such important emphases as religious liberty and ministry of the laity are based on it. Our understanding of church governance and discipleship grows out of it.

But what is the priesthood of all believers? Quite simply it is the conviction that "every Christian is a priest before God and to the world."[1] Being a priest before God means that each one of us stands directly before God with no need for intermediaries. No one tells us what we must believe about God or how we must relate to God. Each of us receives the blessings of salvation and grace directly from God, and each of us is accountable directly to God for our life and faith. Being a priest to the world means that each of us is called by God to a ministry within the world. We are God's representatives, God's agents. As such, we bring God's love to the world.

The priesthood of all believers has particular reference to the relationship between laity and clergy in a Baptist church. It prescribes an equality before God characterized by a shared ministry between laity and ordained clergy. If there is a differentiation between laity and clergy, it is one of *role*, not importance, power, or prestige. When a church ordains a person, it is, in this sense, saying, "We see you are gifted to play a role of leadership within the church. This will be your ministry." In this manner, ordained clergy are not essentially different from the laity; they are just set apart to use particular gifts.

This means that each of us in the church has been given the gift of ministry. All who follow Christ are called to minister on his behalf—in their homes, on their jobs, within the community, and beyond. Although there may be some distinction between the roles of laity and clergy (all members are ministers, not all are pastors), Baptists have no priestly class.

The priesthood of all believers has far-reaching consequences for every Baptist. It means that none of us can be a spectator who sits back while others carry on the work of the church. Nor should any of us be willing to forfeit our responsibilities as ministers and expect the pastor to fulfill them for us. As Baptists, we have no hierarchy within our churches.

## Exploring the Biblical Basis

The Book of Revelation is one of the most difficult Bible books to understand because it is written in a style called apocalyptic writing, which is unfamiliar to many of us. It is difficult to grasp the book's full meaning with great certainty, yet at points it speaks directly and clearly to us about our lives as Christians. The passage that is the

---

### Biblical Basis
Revelation 1:4–6

### Objectives
By the end of the session, participants will be able to:
- define in their own words the meaning of the "priesthood of all believers;"
- identify how they can serve as God's ministers at home, work, church, and in the wider world.

### Key Bible Verse
"[Christ] loves us and freed us from our sins by his blood, and made us to be a kingdom of priests serving his God and Father" (Revelation 1:5–6).

biblical basis for this session is such a point.

Revelation is written as a letter. Our passage comes from the introduction of the letter, which gives the sender's name, the addressees, and a greeting. The letter is from John to the seven churches in Asia. The greeting offers grace and peace in the name of Jesus Christ. As part of the greeting John reminds his readers of what Jesus Christ did for all who believe. Christ loves us and freed us from our sins by his sacrificial death. Building upon the Old Testament concept of the priesthood but expanding it to include all believers, John then states that Christ made us a kingdom of priests. Here we have one of several direct New Testament references to the priesthood of all believers. (The others are found in 1 Peter 2:5,9 and Revelation 5:9–10; 20:6). William Barclay describes it this way: "[John] means that because of what Jesus Christ did, access to the presence of God is not now confined to priests in the narrowest sense of the term, but that it is open to every [person]. Every[one] is a priest. There is a priesthood of all believers. We can come boldly unto the throne of grace (Hebrews 4:16), because for us there is a new and living way into the presence of God."[2] The passage goes on to say that service is a part of our priesthood—serving God, doing the work of God, being involved in ministry.

When these two understandings of priesthood, access and service, are held together, we begin to capture a sense of what the priesthood of all believers is about. John made a grand claim. Israel was quite comfortable with the notion that access and service, priesthood, was appropriate for a select few. To say, however, that it was for *all* believers was a radically new understanding. That radically new understanding of priesthood remains central to the life and thought of Baptists.

## As you prepare for this lesson:
**Pray for each participant by name.**
Ask that God will use this session to speak to the heart of each of your students, that they might experience more fully a direct and personal relationship with God and know better how God can use them in the ministry of Christ's church.

**Read and reflect on the Bible passage** (Revelation 1:4–6). Think about ways in which you have been playing the role of priest in your relationships. What is special about this passage that you would like to pass on to your students?

**Seek input from your pastor.** If possible, ask your pastor to take a few moments before class to complete the activity "Clergy or Laity?" for use with Step 4. Ask for permission to use the pastor's responses during class time or invite the pastor to join the class for discussion of this activity.

## Beginning
**1.** *Introduce the theme.* (5 minutes)
■ Welcome the class, and then write on newsprint or a chalkboard the phrase "priesthood of all believers."
■ Ask volunteers to share what they think the phrase means and why it is or is not important to them.
■ Use the material from "Background for the Leader" to explain to the class the concept of priesthood of all believers.
■ Emphasize that this belief has as much to do with responsibilities as with rights: It means that all Christians stand personally before God without the need for a mediator. It also means that all Christians, laity and clergy alike, are called to serve and minister to others in Jesus' name.

**2.** *Read about and discuss the importance of the "priesthood of all believers." (10 minutes)*
■ Distribute handout #4 and ask the class to turn to "Every Believer a Minister?"
■ Invite a volunteer to read the section aloud.
■ Lead the class in a brief discussion of the questions on the handout.

## Exploring
**3.** *Read and examine the Scripture. (10–15 minutes)*
■ Direct the class to turn to the text in Revelation 1:4–6.
■ Read or use your own words to share some of the background material about the book of Revelation from the section titled "Exploring the Biblical Background."
■ Tell the class that one way to understand this passage is from the perspective of gift and responsibility.
■ Write these two words, *Gift* and *Responsibility,* on newsprint or a chalkboard.
■ Ask class members what gift they believe the passage describes. *(Christ freed us from our sins.)*

■ Then ask what responsibility the passage describes. *(To be priests serving God.)*
■ Ask class members to reflect on ways they experience both the gift and responsibility in their own lives. You may want to add to this discussion by using the material on access and service that is included in "Exploring the Biblical Basis."

**4.** *Define roles and responsibilities of clergy and laity. (10 minutes)*
■ Direct class members to turn to "Clergy or Laity?" on the handout.
■ Review the directions for this activity and give the participants a few minutes to complete it, placing a check in the "Pastor Only," "Laity Only," or "Pastor and Laity" column for each item.
■ When the class has completed the activity, review responses for each item. Is there a unanimity of responses for each item, or are there differences of opinion?

■ Lead the class in a discussion of differences as they arise.
■ If you asked your pastor to complete this activity, share his or her responses with the class at this time.
■ Conclude this step by asking: "What insights can you draw about the priesthood of all believers based on this activity?"

## Responding

**5.** *Identify ways to serve God. (10–15 minutes)*
■ Ask the class to turn to "Responding to God's Call to Ministry."
■ Read Maring and Hudson's statement aloud.
■ Review the directions for this activity, asking class members to take several minutes to write down ways they can serve as God's ministers in each of the settings listed.
■ When everyone has finished, invite volunteers to share one item from each heading.

■ Then ask: "What specific thing can you do this week to be a more effective minister in one or more of the settings in which you represent God?"

**6.** *Close with prayer. (5 minutes)*
■ Give the class a few moments to share comments about the session.
■ Close in prayer, thanking God for the privilege of serving as a minister in the name of Jesus Christ. Ask God to guide and bless the collective ministry of class members as they go out into the world this week, that others will know the wonder of Christ's love.

## Notes
1. Walter B. Shurden, ed., *Proclaiming the Baptist Vision: The Priesthood of All Believers* (Macon, Ga.: Smyth and Helwys, 1993), 2.
2. William Barclay, *The Revelation of John* (Philadelphia: Westminster Press, 1959), 1:44.

# CHAPTER 5

# Religious Liberty

## Background for the Leader

They are two of our greatest legacies—the theological principle of religious liberty and the constitutional doctrine of separation of church and state. Because of Baptists, they are part of America's fabric of life. From early colonial days Baptists have worked to establish and maintain religious freedom.

Maintaining a consistent Baptist witness for freedom hasn't always been easy. Our Baptist forebears were whipped and imprisoned. Even today many advocates of this Baptist emphasis are criticized and ridiculed. When Baptists speak of religious liberty, they mean that decisions about faith and one's relationship with God are up to the individual, not the state.

Baptists believe that the church can maintain its purpose and integrity best if it exists free from government interference, whether supportive or hostile. In this session we will look at a biblical passage in which the early church and its leaders deal with this issue of outside interference. We will also explore some of the important reasons religious freedom continues to be an important concern for us as Baptists. Early Baptists didn't see things in the usual and customary way. They had different notions

than most people about what it meant to be faithful and how to respond to Christ's claims on their lives. They often got into trouble with the authorities, and these experiences shaped the Baptist understanding of religious freedom.

By the grace of God, Baptists forged the experiences of religious persecution into an understanding of religious freedom. In the past, religious persecution had led to the establishment of a new authority that imposed its will on others. Baptists sought to provide freedom for all religious beliefs and expressions.

Baptists have been present whenever religious freedom has been talked about. Roger Williams, although a Baptist for only a few months, was instrumental in establishing Rhode Island as a place of religious freedom and in making Baptists acutely aware of the need for this freedom. Isaac Backus, a Massachusetts Baptist pastor, was a tireless proponent of this same freedom before the Continental Congress in the eighteenth century. John Leland, a Virginia Baptist pastor, played a vitally important role in the effort to secure a Bill of Rights that guaranteed religious freedom. Baptists have also been present whenever religious freedom has been threatened.

Presidents Jefferson and Madison supported the secular rationale for separation of church and state. This view maintains a "high wall of separation"; it prohibits government action from imposing religion in people's lives.

A second rationale for religious freedom is evangelical in its approach. This view is based in our historic Baptist principle of soul freedom. Soul freedom is the right and responsibility of the individual to stand before God and make decisions regarding his or her relationship with God. In this view, the purpose of separation of church and state is not to protect persons *from* religion but to protect them *for* religion. Its purpose is to enable the unfettered development of faith. It seeks to protect both the individual Christian and the church from interference from the state that can thwart vital and vibrant faith.

The secular view of separation, for example, objects to state-mandated prayer out of a concern that prayer not be imposed on those who don't believe in it. The evangelical view of separation objects to state-mandated prayer because it believes firmly in the value, meaning, and power of prayer and refuses to let the state determine what prayer is and when it should happen.

The Baptist view of the need for separation of church and state has placed us in the company of those who have a much more secular view of life than we do. It has opened us to attacks that we are not truly "religious" or that we do not care about faith. But Baptists take faith very seriously. Baptists are suspicious of any apart from the church who would attempt to define what religion is and tell us how to practice it.

## Exploring the Biblical Basis

Peter and John had been in trouble before. Acts 3:1–4:31 tells the story of their arrest for preaching about Christ in the temple and healing a crippled beggar. After spending a night in jail, the two were brought before the council. Facing his accusers, Peter gave an impassioned speech that outlined basic Christian teaching about Christ and his resurrection. He claimed that it was this

power that enabled them to heal the crippled man. Amazed at their boldness but fearful their message would spread, the authorities ordered them to never preach or heal in Jesus' name again. Peter and John replied, "Whether it is right in God's sight to listen to you rather than to God, you must judge; for we cannot keep from speaking about what we have seen and heard" (Acts 4:19–20). They then went home and prayed for boldness. Their prayer was answered, and the apostles returned to the temple to heal and preach.

It wasn't long before the apostles were back in jail. That story is in Acts 5:17–32. This time an angel appeared during the night to set them free. Back to the temple they went. The next morning the council assembled and commanded that the apostles be brought before them. Instead, one of the temple police reported that, even though all the doors were still locked, the prisoners were nowhere to be found. Everyone was stunned. Then more shocking news followed: the men they had jailed were preaching in the temple. Once again the apostles were brought before the council, which demanded that they explain the defiance of their orders. Peter said simply, "We must obey God rather than any human authority" (Acts 5:29).

A number of stories in Acts portray the early church establishing its identity, both as a fellowship of believers and in relationship with the outside world. A feature of these stories is the issue of authority: In what will we trust? Whom will we follow? This passage clearly affirms that no one or no thing except God will determine who we

are or what we do. This stance led directly to the persecution suffered by the early church. It set Christians in direct conflict with religious and political authorities who sought to determine what others should think and do, what they should believe, and how they should worship. Written following the early days of persecution, this passage reflects a central tenet of the church's identity. It affirms the historical reality and the contemporary challenge that to be the church, to be persons and communities of faith, is to owe ultimate allegiance to God.

## As you prepare for this lesson:
### Pray for each participant by name.

Teaching is more than an intellectual exercise. It is an opportunity to enter into the lives of your students in a way that will enable them to grow in faith and relationship with God. Pray that God will help you do that. As you read this material and prepare for class, keep each of the class members in prayer. This may be a topic on which there is disagreement among class members. Be especially prayerful that each may be open to the views of others, so that learning may take place.

**Read and reflect on the Bible passage** (Acts 5:17–32). Read the account of Peter before the council. Be especially attentive to the radical nature of his statement, "We must obey God rather than any human authority." To grasp the impact of what he said, it might be helpful to imagine someone saying the same thing in a courtroom or at a congressional hearing today. How would those in authority respond?

This will be a discussion question in class, so it will be helpful if you have thought about it. Also consider the meaning of such a statement for us today. Is the need to speak and live with the boldness Peter showed less for us because we live in a nation that allows religious freedom?

Acts 3:1–4:31 provides important background information on this passage. It will be helpful for you to read this in order to understand the events that led up to the incident described in Acts 5.

**Review the rationales for separation of church and state.** Review the secular and evangelical perspectives on the need for separation of church and state so that you can help the class understand them. Several resources are suggested in Step 5. If you can order these before the session, class time can be used to explore and share about the resources. See the handout for ordering information.

**Select an appropriate hymn or song to close the class.** Several hymns are suggested in Step 6.

## Beginning

1. *List reactions to key words. (5 minutes)*
■ Welcome class members and make introductions as needed.
■ Tell the class members that the focus of this session is the historic Baptist principle of religious liberty.
■ Explain that to begin the session you would like them to respond to a number of key phrases that are often used in discussions about this topic.
■ Explain that you will state a phrase and they will call out any associations and reactions they

have. The phrases are: religious liberty, First Amendment, separation of church and state, and school prayer. Write the phrases on newsprint or the chalkboard to refer to later in the session.

## Exploring

2. *Read and reflect on the passage. (10 minutes)*
■ Ask class members to turn to Acts 5:17–32 in their Bibles. The first paragraph of "Exploring the Biblical Basis" will help provide the background for the events that are described here. Material relevant to the story is found in Acts 3:1–4:31.
■ Ask a class member to read Acts 5:17–32 aloud.
■ Use the following questions to guide a discussion:
— What were the concerns of the Sadducees?
— What were they afraid of?
— Why were they furious at Peter's claim, "We must obey God rather than any human authority"?
— What do you think the response would be today if this same claim were made before political authorities? religious authorities?
— If everyone did what Peter advocates, what would be the basis for order in society?
■ Explain to the class that the issues raised in this passage are very similar to those raised in the discussion over the separation of church and state.
■ Note that Baptists support this principle because they believe "we must obey God rather than any human authority."
■ Explain that when early Baptists made this claim they received the

same kind of fury the Sadducees demonstrated. The fear behind this fury was a concern about what the basis for order in society would be. People simply could not conceive of an orderly society without common religious beliefs and practice.
■ Tell the class that the remainder of the session will be used to consider how this passage relates to the current debate about separation of church and state, especially as it applies to the issue of school prayer.

3. *Consider two perspectives on separation of church and state. (10–15 minutes)*
■ Distribute handout #5 to the class members.
■ Read aloud or summarize "Religious Liberty and the Separation of Church and State." The first paragraph draws the distinction between the theological principle of religious freedom and the political doctrine of separation of church and state. The second paragraph mentions three Baptists who were important participants in the early discussion of religious liberty and separation of church and state.
■ Ask a class member to read aloud "Two Perspectives on the Separation of Church and State," which describes the secular and evangelical rationales.
■ Ask class members to express the differences between the two perspectives in their own words.
■ Share the illustration related to government-mandated prayer that is included in "Background for the Leader" to help them see the differences more concretely.
■ On newsprint or the chalkboard, create a chart that describes the differences between the perspectives.

Encourage class members to offer their suggestions on this. Possibilities that might be included in the chart are:

### The secular perspective . . .
— is neutral/skeptical toward faith
— seeks to protect individuals from religion
— wants to limit religious interference with the individual
— is concerned about individual rights
— advocates clear separation of church and state

### The evangelical perspective . . .
— is positive toward faith
— seeks to protect individuals for faith
— wants to limit governmental interference with religion and personal faith
— is concerned about faithful living
— advocates clear separation of church and state

■ Review the items in the chart with class members.
■ Note that the actual differences between the two are not as absolute as indicated here. For example, the evangelical perspective does value individual rights even though it is more concerned about faithful living.

**4.** *Read and react to a statement about school prayer.*
*(10–20 minutes)*
■ Ask the class members to read "The School Prayer Amendment" found in the handout. They may read silently, or ask a class member to read it aloud as others follow along.
■ Explain that it is an article that appeared in a church newsletter.
■ Use the questions following the article to guide a discussion of it.

## Responding
**5.** *Discover additional resources and action possibilities. (5 minutes)*

■ Ask class members to look at the list of additional resources and action possibilities that are listed on the handout.
■ Encourage class members to take responsibility for learning more about religious liberty issues by following up on one of the items that are listed.

**6.** *Close with a song and prayer.*
*(5 minutes)*
■ Invite the class to sing a familiar hymn that lifts up the challenge of obeying God rather than human authority. Possibilities include "I Have Decided to Follow Jesus," "God of Grace and God of Glory," and "Stand Up, Stand Up for Jesus."
■ Close the session with a prayer offering thanks to God for the gift of religious liberty and asking God for the strength and courage needed to continue the work our Baptist forebears began.

# CHAPTER 6

# Autonomy of the Local Church

## Background for the Leader

Baptists have a different understanding of the church than most people do. For us the local congregation is the key because it is representative of the whole church of Jesus Christ. It is free to govern its own affairs, to order its worship, to decide how and with what other churches it will relate. Baptists call this freedom "congregational autonomy." Yet Baptist churches are not just isolated congregations. From the earliest times we have seen the need to gather in associations to do things we cannot do alone and to seek counsel and advice from one another. At times these two realities have created tension among us as we have sought to balance them appropriately in the midst of sometimes contentious issues. The principles remain valid, however; and it is those principles that are the focus of this session.

Congregational autonomy is, in the words of William Keucher, former president of the American Baptist Churches in the U.S.A., "the right of each congregation (1) to choose its own ministers and officers, (2) to establish its own covenant membership and discipline and confessions, (3) to order its life in its own organizational forms with its constitution and bylaws, (4) to implement its right to belong to other denominational agencies and ecumenical church bodies, (5) to own and to control its own property and budget."[1]

More recently historian Walter Shurden has affirmed several of these points and lifted up some new ones. He writes in his book *The Baptist Identity: Four Fragile Freedoms,* "Church freedom is the historic Baptist affirmation that local churches are free, under the lordship of Jesus Christ, to determine their membership and leadership, to order their worship and work, to ordain whom they perceive as gifted for ministry, male or female, and to participate in the larger Body of Christ, of whose unity and mission Baptists are proudly a part."[2]

This means that every Baptist congregation has the freedom to be the church it believes God has called it to be. And as is always the case, with the freedom comes a great responsibility—to listen and respond to God's call to be the church in a particular time and place.

First, let's deal with the freedom. The Baptist concept of the church is grounded in the concrete reality of the local congregation. That congregation is free to determine its corporate life and its relationships with others. We believe that it is this grounding that brings life to the church and enables it to faithfully respond to God's call to ministry both within its own walls and to the world. No predetermined hierarchical system dictates to congregations.

## Biblical Basis
Acts 2:40–47

## Objectives
By the end of the session participants will be able to:
■ describe key elements of the Baptist principle of congregational autonomy;
■ describe ways in which their church can and does live out the responsibility of its freedom.

## Key Bible Verse
"They devoted themselves to the apostles' teaching and fellowship, to the breaking of bread and prayers" (Acts 2:42).

There are no bishops, no outside controlling groups. Each congregation can set its standards for membership, determine its structure and organization, choose its style of worship. Certainly there is much in common among Baptist churches in these areas, but each congregation is free to change as it understands God's will for itself.

Included in this freedom is the freedom to relate to other churches through denominational and ecumenical structures. As part of these relationships, the structures may set additional criteria for membership and participation. At times there is significant debate over what those criteria should be. Once they are decided, however, each congregation retains its right to determine whether or not to continue in relationship with those structures. That freedom is a given, the very core of congregational autonomy.

With this freedom, however, comes the great responsibility of being the church—of listening for and responding to God's call so that the congregation will remain faithful in its life and ministry. No one can tell a local Baptist congregation what it must be and do except God. The congregation's responsibility is to listen and obey when God speaks. Thus, each local congregation needs to develop a listening stance, refusing to be so caught up in its own issues and survival that it cannot hear God's voice. It must constantly be open to change, willing to move in new directions when God calls, and willing to risk seeing and doing things differently from others in obedience to God's will. Each congregation must bear its own responsibility rather than relying on bishops or outside structures to tell it how to be faithful.

## Exploring the Biblical Basis

The Bible passage for this session is the first description of a church in the New Testament. Although only a few verses, it tells us much about the nature of the church and the life of a local congregation.

The story picks up immediately following the gift of the Holy Spirit at Pentecost. Peter has preached a great sermon proclaiming the Good News of Jesus Christ. Many believe. Those who do are gathered into a community of faith that is the church.

Key Baptist principles about the church are illustrated in this biblical passage.

*The church is a community of believers* (v. 41). Baptists call it "regenerate church membership." This means that only those who have experienced the saving and transforming power of Jesus Christ in their lives are ready for membership.

*Baptism is the introductory rite of membership* (v. 41). Those who believed were baptized and became members of the church. This is one of several biblical reference points for our belief in believer's baptism.

*Learning, fellowship, worship, and prayer are essential elements of congregational life* (vv. 42, 46–47). These words, although not all-inclusive, are the first that describe congregational life in the early church. They still inform us about the important elements of congregational life today.

*Wondrous things happen within the fellowship of the church* (v. 43).

The passage refers to them as "wonders and signs." They testify to a faith in the great things that happen when two or three are gathered together in the name of Christ.

*There is a great intimacy of sharing within the congregation* (vv. 44–45). The passage speaks of everyone selling their possessions and holding everything in common. While most churches do not follow that practice today, it is an appropriate image for the depth of commitment to one another that is to be found within a congregation.

*As powerful as this community experience is for those who share it, there is always an openness to others, a desire to incorporate new believers whom God provides* (vv. 41, 47). The power of the gospel and the love that is evident in the community attract others, and the congregation is always open to receive them.

From the New Testament perspective all of this happens within the context of the local congregation. There are no church structures and hierarchies. These words, which are used to describe the very first church, are words that shape the life and faith of local congregations.

## As you prepare for this lesson:

**Pray for each participant by name.**
Each member of your class attaches some meaning to church as it is made real for them in the local congregation. For some these meanings may be very positive; others may have decidedly mixed feelings about the church and your congregation. As you pray for your students, focus on their experiences

of church. Pray that through this session they may develop a clearer understanding of the freedom and responsibility of being the church together.

**Read and reflect on the Bible passage** (Acts 2:40–47). Use the material in "Exploring the Biblical Basis" to guide your reflection on the passage. Consider ways in which you have experienced each of these principles in your own life and congregation. Reflect on the elements that are missing in your own life and how that might be changed. To get a full picture of the context of this passage, you may want to read the story of Pentecost, which begins in Acts 2:1.

**Review church relationships.** For Step 5, ask your pastor or other church leader to name denominational and ecumenical relationships your church maintains if you don't know them already.

# Beginning

**1.** *Share experiences of "church."* *(5–10 minutes)*
■ Welcome class members.
■ Explain to them that in this session you will be focusing on the Baptist understanding of the church.
■ Point out that it is one way in which we are significantly different from many other churches.
■ Use words such as these to introduce this step: "All of us have some understanding of 'church' that we carry around in our heads. We know what a church is, or at least is supposed to be. We know times in our lives when we have experienced the reality of church, and often this has had a profound impact on us. Maybe we can't

define it, but we know it when we see it and experience it."
■ Ask class members to share experiences from their own lives in which they had a special sense of the church being an important and profound reality for them.
■ Thank class members for their willingness to share these important experiences in their lives.
■ Encourage them to keep this image of the church in their minds as they work through today's session.

**2.** *Introduce the principle of congregational autonomy. (5 minutes)*
■ Distribute handout #6.
■ Explain that one of the most important of Baptist principles is congregational autonomy.
■ Read over the description of congregational autonomy. You may want to use information from "Background for the Leader" to add to the description.
■ Check to see that everyone has a basic understanding of what this term means.

# Exploring

**3.** *Investigate a biblical church. (10–15 minutes)*
■ Ask class members to turn to Acts 2:40–47 in their Bibles.
■ Set the scene for this story by explaining that it describes what happened immediately following the gift of the Holy Spirit at Pentecost. If class members need more background, read or summarize Acts 2:1–16,37–39 (verses 17–36 are the text of Peter's sermon).
■ Write this phrase on the chalkboard or a sheet of newsprint: "This passage tells me that the church . . ."

■ Explain that as you read the passage you would like them to stop you any time they hear in it a description of an important quality of this very first church.
■ Provide an example such as this: Verse 41, "So those who welcomed his message were baptized . . . ," tells us the church was composed of people who responded to God's Word and decided to be baptized.
■ Read the passage, encouraging class members to stop you any time they would like to make a comment. The material in "Exploring the Biblical Basis" provides information on some of the major points about the church that are made in this passage.
■ If class members do not respond immediately to those points, encourage them to look at each specific verse and determine what quality is described in it.

**4.** *Examine three styles of church organization. (5 minutes)*
■ Say, "With this as background, let's now look at three basic ways in which churches today are organized. All three models have a biblical foundation, but see which one you believe responds best to the description of the church we have just read."
■ Ask class members to turn to "Three Ways of Organizing the Church."
■ Divide the class into three smaller groups.
■ Ask each group to read the description of one of the ways and decide which of the three diagrams best symbolizes it. The answers are:
  — Congregational: C
  — Presbyterian: A
  — Episcopal: B

- When all have finished, bring the class back together and have the members of each group share the logo they selected and the reasons for their choice. If two groups chose the same logo, discuss the choices with the entire class to see if a consensus can be reached on which logo is most appropriate.

**5.** *Explore relationships with others. (10 minutes)*
- Ask class members to turn to "The Way We Relate."
- Review the list of possible relationships found there.
- Ask class members to check the relationships that they know their church has and fill in each blank with the specific name.
- Invite them to add any additional relationships that the church may have. (Supplement their list with relationships you learned about before the class session.)
- When the class has finished this work ask, "Does the fact that we are involved in all these relationships with other churches mean

we aren't really practicing congregational autonomy?"
- Help the class understand that relating with others is compatible with congregational autonomy and that Baptists have practiced both from our earliest days.
- Emphasize that what makes us autonomous even in these relationships is that every congregation retains the right to decide to whom it will relate.

**6.** *Discover the responsibility that goes with freedom. (5–10 minutes)*
- Ask the class members to turn to "The Responsibility That Goes with Freedom."
- Ask a volunteer to read it aloud.
- Use these questions to guide a class discussion:
  — In what ways do you see us as a congregation exercising that responsibility?
  — How is this different than it would be for a Presbyterian or Episcopal church?
  — What are the things that get in the way of our hearing and responding to God's call?

  — What might we do to be even more responsible in our attention to God's will for us as a congregation?

## Responding
**7.** *Close with a hymn and prayer. (5 minutes)*
- Invite the class to join in singing a hymn that celebrates the church, such as "The Church's One Foundation" or "I Love Thy Kingdom, Lord."
- Close with a prayer thanking God for the great gift of the church and asking for the courage and insight needed to use our freedom responsibly by always seeking to attune ourselves to God's will for the church.

## Notes
1. William H. Kuecher, "Congregational Autonomy," *Baptist Leader*, March 1976, 49.
2. Walter B. Shurden, *The Baptist Identity: Four Fragile Freedoms* (Macon, Ga.: Smyth and Helwys, 1993), 33.

# CHAPTER 7

# Ministry of the Laity

## Background for the Leader

Ministry of the laity is part of our Baptist tradition. Yet some people believe that one of the greatest challenges facing the church today is the need to rework the relationship between clergy and laity. This view is forcefully presented by church consultant Loren Mead in his book *Five Challenges for the Once and Future Church*.[1] Mead argues that an important part of meeting that challenge will be the development of a better understanding of the role of the laity as those who have a ministry both within the church and in the world.

Our purpose in this session is to explore the ministry of the laity—its tradition and its biblical foundation—and understand more fully what it means for us. As we do this, we'll discover that this important principle impacts a great variety of issues that have to do with church governance and leadership. It has great implications for the appropriate role of clergy, influences the way we approach pastoral care within the congregation, and shapes our understanding of who does mission work and how it is done. As you look at this issue, focus on God's call as it comes to each disciple and its impact in shaping each person's ministry.

The phrase "ministry of the laity" conjures up a wide variety of images in people's minds. One view suggests that laity can and should play an active part in the church's ministry by serving on boards and committees, making budget decisions, and leading in worship. The focus of ministry is inside. It can include jobs some churches hire paid staff to do but which others leave to the laity.

A more expansive and more biblically appropriate understanding of ministry of the laity begins with the recognition that all disciples of Jesus Christ have a ministry to which they are called. For some that ministry is inside the church; for many more it is outside. The ministries to which laity are called are both within the church and in the world.

Ministry of the laity also affirms the importance of participation of the laity in what are often seen as clergy responsibilities. They share in pastoral care as well as in leadership in worship. They preside at the Lord's Table, offering prayers of thanks and blessing for the bread and cup. They respond to God's call to minister to others—children, youth, and adults, who are a part of the community of faith—in ways similar to the care extended to widows and orphans by the early church. They nurture one another in the faith and in their relationship with Christ. They become "priests" to one another.

Ministry of the laity affirms the ministry each disciple has in the world. In these various ministries we use our God-given gifts as we respond to God's call to serve others in the name of Christ. The particular nature of the ministry varies greatly. It may be within the family as mother or father. It may be job-related, serving others in a business or a profession. It may be a call to volunteer service, providing needed support to the community and its members. It may be a call that has political implications or that leads

---

## Biblical Basis

Ephesians 4:1–7,11–13

## Objectives

By the end of the session participants will be able to:
- describe the Baptist concept of ministry of the laity;
- discuss ways in which this concept influences the ministry of the church.

## Key Bible Verse

". . . for the work of ministry, for building up the body of Christ . . ." (Ephesians 4:12).

to social action. Whatever its exact form, it begins with a stirring in the heart, as a sense of calling from God. When we are open, the Holy Spirit directs us into a particular role, not just because we want to be there, but because we believe that this is what God intends for us to do.

This understanding of the ministry of the laity is grounded in our Baptist principle of the priesthood of all believers. That principle maintains that each person stands before God; no roles elevate some above others. All can go directly to God and have a personal relationship with God without the need for another person to intercede. In the same way, all are called by God. Each one of us is called to a ministry that uses the gifts God has given us. Each of us has both the freedom and the responsibility to exercise that ministry.

The implications for the congregation of this understanding of ministry of the laity are significant. This principle emphasizes the importance of the congregational role in helping members discover, develop, and use their gifts; it implies that sensitivity to God's call is a primary concern for all Christians; and it suggests that churches value their members' gifts and response to God's call to minister as laity in the church and the world!

## Exploring the Biblical Basis

The New Testament offers no clear description or definition of ministry of the laity, because there was no formalized process of ordination, no separation of clergy and laity in the early church. Passages such as

Ephesians 4:1–7,11–13, however, provide a solid underpinning for this historic Baptist principle. They affirm three basic concepts that continue to be important for us today: (1) Christ gave a variety of gifts; (2) these gifts are to be used to enable others in ministry; and (3) this ministry belongs to all the people of God, both clergy and laity, and takes place both inside and outside the church.

The concern of the Letter to the Ephesians is nothing less than the redemption of all creation. You can't get much bigger in scope than that! In the letter's view, this is God's plan; it is also what the work of Christ was and is all about. As the body of Christ, the church continues that work. This is where the ministry of the laity comes in. The ministry of the *laos*, the people of God, is to join in the work of redemption, not just of themselves, but of all creation. This is easier said than done. After this bold affirmation in Ephesians 1, much of the rest of the letter explains how this happens through the church and in the lives of Christians.

Our focus passage in this session comes from the section of the letter that deals with the church. The writer first acknowledges the call that comes to all Christians and encourages his readers to remain faithful to that call (4:1). He then affirms our unity in Christ: "one Lord, one faith, one baptism, one God and Father of all, who is above all and through all and in all" (4:5). This unity, however, is not sameness, for there is variety in the church, specifically a variety of gifts. In Ephesians these gifts are seen as different roles that are played in the church: some are

apostles, some prophets, some evangelists, some pastors and teachers. All these are essential if the church is to fulfill its purpose. These roles exist "to equip the saints for the work of ministry, for building up the body of Christ" (4:12). Remember, the meaning of saints here is broader than simply those special people who have a particularly high degree of holiness or who have enabled miracles. It is the term used to describe all who have claimed Jesus Christ as their Lord and Savior, much as we might use the term believer or disciple.

The meaning of this phrase, then, is that the various gifts exist so that disciples will be equipped to do the work of the church, for "ministry, for building up the body of Christ." These are really two sides of the same coin. Ministry and building up the body of Christ are so intimately tied together that they cannot be separated. The place and nature of this work entail a wide range of possibilities.

At the time the letter was written, there was no clear notion of ordination. The specific roles mentioned in the passage were for everyone, not just clergy. Any of the *laos* might be in the role of apostle, prophet, evangelist, pastor, or teacher. The key was whether or not they had the specific gifts needed to fulfill these roles. The primary focus of prophets, pastors, and teachers was most often inside the church. That of the apostles and evangelists, however, was most often outside. Similarly, the ministry of the saints could be both within the church or to the community and world. All of it was and is ministry. All of it led and leads to building up the body of Christ.

## As you prepare for this lesson:

**Pray for each participant by name.** Think about the gifts and ministries of the people in your class. Can you identify them for each person? Do you see evidence that they themselves are aware of the gifts God has given them? Are their lives focused on using those gifts to do the work of Christ in the church and in the world? As you pray, offer to God the gifts and ministry of each person in your class. Pray that the students may be more aware of their giftedness and ways in which they can faithfully participate in the work of Christ.

**Read and reflect on the Bible passage** (Ephesians 4:1–7,11–13). The fourth chapter of Ephesians is one of the more familiar passages among the New Testament letters. Don't let this familiarity keep you from prayerful reflection on it. If you have time, you may want to read the entire letter. If this is not possible, reading chapters 1–4 will help provide a setting for the specific passage used in the session.

## Beginning

**1.** *Share ministries. (5 minutes)*
■ Welcome class members.
■ After everyone is settled ask, "What's your ministry?" If there is no response, ask it again.
■ If there is still no response, rephrase the question, asking something such as, "In what areas of your life do you have a special sense of doing God's work?"
■ Encourage people to share. As they do, keep mental track of the types of responses they make. How many are related to work in the church? at home? in volunteer serv-

ice? on the job? How many people talk about the use of God-given gifts? about serving others?
■ After everyone has shared, give some feedback to the class based on what you have heard. Include such things as the ease or difficulty with which people were able to talk about ministry, places it happens, and whom it is directed toward.

**2.** *Define "ministry of the laity."* *(5–10 minutes)*
■ Explain to the class that the focus of this session is ministry of the laity, an important Baptist emphasis.
■ Point out that this concept has been important in our thinking about the church and discipleship from the very beginning of our history and has become a renewed interest recently.
■ Write the phrase *Ministry of the Laity* on the chalkboard or newsprint.
■ Ask class members to offer definitions and descriptions.
■ Write key words and phrases on the chalkboard or newsprint.
■ After all have shared, ask the class to decide which are the most important elements of a definition. Take a minute or two to write the definition on the chalkboard or newsprint.
■ Tell the class that this is a preliminary definition and that they will come back to it again at the end of the session and consider ways they might revise it.

## Exploring

**3.** *Do a Bible study.* *(5–10 minutes)*
■ Distribute handout #7.
■ Ask class members to turn to Ephesians 4 in their Bibles.

■ Explain that the passage you will be looking at in this session is a brief section of the Letter to the Ephesians.
■ Ask someone in the class to read, from the handout, the background material on the letter and passage.
■ Introduce the reading of the passage by noting that at this point the letter is focused on the nature of the church.
■ Point out verse 4, which is a great affirmation of the unity of the church.
■ Explain that the letter goes on to discuss the diversity that is found in the midst of this unity. Note that this diversity is based in the variety of gifts that Christ has given.
■ Ask someone in the class to read verses 1–7 and 11–13. Mention that the verses that are not included here contain a difficult-to-understand allusion to Psalm 68 that does not influence the meaning of the passage.
■ After the passage has been read, point out the phrase in verse 1: "lead a life worthy of the calling to which you have been called."
■ Explain that one way to understand this passage is that it describes the beginning steps in leading such a life.
■ Ask class members, based on what they know about the theme of Ephesians in general and this passage in particular, to name the calling to which the passage refers. This discussion should affirm two main points: 1) In a general sense, the calling is one to all Christians to participate in God's plan for the redemption of creation. 2) Specifically, it is a calling for each individual Christian to use his or her gifts in particular ways in ministry. If class members do not bring up these

24

points, refer to them yourself as you draw the discussion to a close.

**4.** *Reflect on ministries.*
*(10 minutes)*
- Tell the class members that they are now going to learn about a person from our Baptist history who illustrates several ways in which the call to ministry can be fulfilled.
- Ask them to turn to look at the section on Helen Barrett Montgomery on the handout, and invite someone in the class read it aloud.
- When the reader has finished, use these questions to guide a discussion:
  — What specific ministries did Helen Barrett Montgomery pursue?
  — Which of these took place inside the church? which outside?
  — How are all these activities "ministry"?
  — Do you think she was "called" to these ministries in the same way clergy are called? If so, why? If not, how was it different?

**5.** *Consider personal calls and ministries. (10 minutes)*
- Restate the question with which you began the class: "What's your ministry?"
- Ask class members to reflect on it again in light of the Bible study and discussion about Helen Barrett Montgomery.

- Ask: "Do you have a different idea of your ministry now?"
- Invite class members to think about the ministry of others in the class.
- Tell them that sometimes others can give us important insight into our true calling and ministry.
- Encourage them to share about the calling and ministry they believe others in the class have. This can be an important time of affirming one another and helping each other understand their ministry more fully.
- If you think the class members may find it difficult to do this sharing personally, distribute index cards and ask them to use a separate card for each person for whom they want to write an affirmation. Collect the cards, read them aloud, and distribute them to the appropriate class members.
- Return to the definition of ministry of the laity you developed in Step 2.
- Ask class members if they want to make any changes in it. Discuss suggested changes and make them on the newsprint or chalkboard.

## Responding

**6.** *Consider the implications of ministry of the laity. (5–10 minutes)*
- Ask participants to turn to the section entitled "Ministry of the Laity" on the handout.

- Note the titles of each of the three paragraphs.
- Have someone different read each of the paragraphs.
- After each paragraph is read, discuss these questions:
  — With what statements do you agree/disagree?
  — How fully is this practiced in our church?
  — What could we do to be better at it?
- Draw the discussion to a close by summarizing the main points that have been made. If there is a strong consensus for doing something related to ministry of the laity in your church, ask the class to consider what steps could be taken next.

**7.** *Close with prayer. (5 minutes)*
- Ask class members to offer prayer concerns and affirmations related to their own calling and ministry or the calling and ministry of others in the class.
- Close with a time of prayer offering these concerns to God and thanking God for the honor and joy of being able to participate in ministry.

## Note
1. Loren Mead, *Five Challenges for the Once and Future Church* (Bethesda, Md.: Alban Institute, 1996), 1–15.

# CHAPTER 8

# Discipleship

## Background for the Leader

Christians believe in discipleship—that is, they believe that all who claim faith in Jesus Christ are called to learn about and follow in the way Christ teaches. Baptists, however, bring another dimension to this common belief. Baptists believe in the priesthood of all believers. This notion, that we all have both direct access to God and a ministry from God, makes discipleship an important part of our life and faith. It is through discipleship that our priestly role is developed and our ministry lived out.

A disciple of Jesus Christ seeks to learn more about Jesus and to practice what is learned each day. Discipleship is about knowing Christ, having a significant relationship with him, and living the way Christ would live. Discipleship incorporates all of our life—our being, our knowing, and our doing. This call to discipleship is set against the Baptist focus on the priesthood of believers. Because God calls each one of us to a ministry, part of growing as a disciple is discovering and living out that call.

One way to understand discipleship is to think of it as three pieces of the same pie. Each slice is different, yet each one is connected to the other, and each one has pretty much the same ingredients as the other. The three pieces of the "discipleship pie" are *deepening spiritual life, equipping,* and *ministering.*

*Deepening spiritual life* speaks about the need for disciples to continue to grow in their personal relationship with Christ. Relationships always require work. A relationship with Christ is no different. In fact, in some ways, it may be more difficult because there is no flesh-and-blood person with whom we can sit down across a table and talk. What's great about this relationship is that Christ constantly seeks us out. Christ constantly loves us. Christ constantly desires to have a relationship with us. Spiritual disciplines are the ways Christians traditionally seek to grow in their relationship with Jesus. From prayer to action, from meditation to Bible study, these disciplines are all about strengthening our relationship with Christ. As our relationship with Christ is strengthened, our spiritual life is deepened.

*Equipping* speaks of the need to continue to develop the attributes that make faithful living possible. For Christians a key to equipping is found in the discovery and development of our God-given gifts.

These gifts are given for ministry, to live out our lives as disciples of Jesus Christ. Being equipped, then, is the ongoing process of discovering and developing our gifts. Other important aspects of equipping include acquiring both knowledge and skills. To be disciples of Jesus Christ, we need to know who he is, what he teaches, and how we are to live. That knowledge comes primarily through Bible study. Living as faithful disciples may also require the use of particular skills, such as preaching, leadership, working with groups, carpentry,

---

### Biblical Basis
Colossians 1:27–29

### Objectives
By the end of the session participants will be able to:
■ describe key elements of the lifelong process of discipleship;
■ state one area of discipleship in which they would like to grow in the coming months.

### Key Bible Verse
". . . to bring each one into God's presence as a mature individual in union with Christ" (Colossians 1:28, TEV).

or cooking. The list is limitless and depends on the way in which we have been called to live out our discipleship.

*Ministering* speaks of the need to put faith into action. We do this when we respond to God's call to serve others in the name of Jesus Christ. The deepening spiritual life and the equipping both have a purpose—involvement in ministry as Christ's disciples. In ministering we are fulfilling our call and continuing to grow as disciples of Christ.

## Exploring the Biblical Basis

Paul was in prison. Before him stood the stark reality that he might be put to death because of his work. He used this time to reflect on his life and ministry—the things he had been about and that were most important to him. The section of the Letter to the Colossians that is the biblical basis for this session comes from this part of his reflection.

In Colossians 1:24 (TEV) Paul talks about his suffering. He rejoices in it because it completes the suffering of Christ. As Christ suffered for the church, so Paul suffers for the church. His imprisonment is directly related to the work of the church. That work is, in a word, discipleship. It is bringing "each one into God's presence as a mature individual in union with Christ" (Colossians 1:28, TEV). The Greek word translated "mature" can also be translated "complete." We become mature as we complete God's intentions for us. This happens, Paul claims, through the proclamation of the "secret" that God has now

revealed to everyone. The secret is this: "Christ is in you, which means that you will share the glory of God" (Colossians 1:27, TEV).

Through this indwelling Christ we become mature, and the work of discipleship is accomplished. For Paul this is an ongoing process. In his letter to the Philippians he refers to a race that is being run but is not yet completed (Philippians 3:12–14). Ephesians speaks of the time in the future when we will become "mature [people], reaching to the very height of Christ's full stature" (Ephesians 4:13, TEV). For now, however, the challenge is to keep growing as disciples.

Later in this section of Colossians Paul writes about how that happens. These verses are not included in the Bible basis for this session, but they are important to understanding the work of discipleship. "Since you have accepted Christ Jesus as Lord, live in union with him. Keep your roots deep in him, build your lives on him, and become ever stronger in your faith, as you were taught" (Colossians 2:6–7, TEV). These few words are rich in insights about discipleship.

**1.** Discipleship begins with our acceptance of Christ as Lord. Certainly we learn about being a disciple before then. What we learn helps us commit to Christ, but the actual process of discipleship begins once we have said yes to Christ's call and claim on our lives.

**2.** The central feature of discipleship is learning to live in union with Christ. This is possible because Christ already dwells in us. We fulfill that union when we recognize it and begin to order our lives around it.

**3.** Keeping our roots deep in Christ is what enables the first element of discipleship as described in "Background for the Leader." This is what deepening spiritual life is all about.

**4.** The other two elements of discipleship, equipping and ministering, are encompassed in building our lives on Christ. This includes how we live out our faith in our relationships and what we choose to do with our lives.

**5.** Discipleship is not just sit-down-and-listen teaching. It also includes the teaching that comes from living our lives alongside other disciples and following Jesus as the model of what it means to be truly mature.

## As you prepare for this lesson:
**Pray for each participant by name.**
Discipleship is important for everyone in your class. Those who have made a commitment to Christ in baptism are already disciples. They need to be nurtured in their knowledge of what it means to be a disciple and their ability to live as one. Those who have not yet made this commitment to Christ can begin to understand more fully what such a commitment means as they explore discipleship in this session. As you pray, focus on where each of your students is in his or her relationship with Christ.

**Read and reflect on the Bible passage** (Colossians 1:27–29). You may want to read the entire section this passage is taken from, Colossians 1:24–2:5, which will give you a better sense of the context. Also, read Colossians 2:5–6 and consider its insights into the process of discipleship. Take time to reflect on the key elements that you believe are involved in being mature in Christ. How do you demonstrate these in your own life? What are the points at which you, personally, need to grow as a disciple of Christ?

## Beginning

**1.** *Do sentence completions.*
*(5–10 minutes)*
■ Welcome the class members.
■ Explain that in this session you will be looking at ways in which we continue to grow as disciples of Jesus Christ throughout our lives.
■ As an introduction to this topic, ask the class members to complete this sentence: "The time in my life I felt most alive spiritually was . . . ."
■ When all who wish to do so have shared, ask the class members to complete this second sentence: "Right now the best part of my life as a disciple of Jesus Christ is . . . ." If needed, stimulate discussion by sharing your own sentence completions with the class.

## Exploring

**2.** *Describe a disciple of Jesus Christ. (5–10 minutes)*
■ Share this definition of a disciple with the class: "A disciple is a person who seeks to learn more about and follow more fully the teaching and way of life of another." It will be helpful if you write this definition on newsprint or the chalkboard, or distribute handout #8 at this point so class members can read this definition there.
■ Ask class members how this applies to disciples of Jesus Christ.

■ Ask them to share ways in which Jesus' initial disciples and we today can both (1) learn more about Jesus and (2) follow him more fully. Write these on newsprint or the chalkboard as they are shared.

**3.** *Reflect on the Bible passage.*
*(10 minutes)*
■ Ask class members to turn to Colossians 1:27–29 in their Bibles.
■ Use the information in the first paragraph of "Exploring the Biblical Basis" to explain the setting in which this passage was written.
■ Ask a class member to read the passage aloud. If possible, use the Today's English Version (Good News Bible) translation.
■ Point out that the phrase "mature individuals in union with Christ" is one way to talk about the goal of discipleship.
■ Ask class members what some of the qualities and characteristics of such a "mature" person would be. List these on newsprint or the chalkboard as they are named.
■ Ask: "What do you think makes this maturity possible?"
■ As class members share their thoughts, direct their attention to the passage in order to discover insights that it provides. Point out especially the phrase in verse 27: "And the secret is that Christ is in you . . ."
■ Ask class members what that phrase means to them and how they experience its reality in their own lives.

**4.** *Consider areas of discipleship.*
*(15–20 minutes)*
■ Point out that the sense of personal relationship with Christ that

this phrase describes is a vital element of discipleship.
■ Explain that looking at it and two other qualities will help them get a better handle on what it means to be a disciple.
■ Distribute handout #8, if you haven't already done so.
■ Divide the class into three smaller groups.
■ Introduce the three elements of discipleship with words such as these from "Background for the Leader": "One way to understand discipleship is to think of it as three pieces of the same pie—each different, yet each one connected to the others and each one having much the same ingredients as the others. The three pieces of the 'discipleship pie' are deepening spiritual life, equipping, and ministering."
■ Ask each group to take one of the three elements of discipleship, read the material about it, discuss the questions, and prepare to share their learning with the class.
■ When the groups have completed their preparation, bring the class back together and ask each group to report.
■ Suggest that the class members take notes about each element in the first column of the chart on the handout.
■ After each group's report, allow time for questions and discussion.

## Responding

**5.** *Decide on areas of growth.*
*(5 minutes)*
■ Ask class members to take a few minutes working alone to complete the Discipleship Growth Chart.
■ Explain that in the second column, they are to list those things

they are already doing related to the element of discipleship listed.

■ Explain that in the third column, they should list things that they believe they could do but are not currently doing. They might also include in this column things they are currently doing that they would like to do better or more completely.

■ When they have finished this reflection, ask them to complete the sentence under the chart as a way to set a specific goal for their own growth as a disciple of Jesus Christ.

**6.** *Close with a prayer and a hymn. (5 minutes)*

■ Bring the class together for a closing prayer.

■ Explain that you will begin the prayer and then allow time for them to offer a sentence, sharing the goal they have set for themselves in Step 5.

■ Use words such as these to begin: "Loving God, you have called each one of us to be a disciple of your Son, Jesus Christ. We have heard that call and responded. That is why we are here, why we seek to live our lives in service to you. That is also why we strive to grow as your disciples. Hear us now as we share the ways in which we want to grow, seeking your support and strength to do so . . . ."

■ Allow time for class members to share, and then conclude the prayer with words such as these: "You know us, God—the words that we have spoken and the words that are in our hearts. You know who we are and what you want us to be. Help each one of us to live today and every day as people who truly are disciples of your Son. Amen."

■ Close the session by singing a hymn of discipleship such as, "I Have Decided to Follow Jesus," or "Take My Life and Let It Be."

# CHAPTER 9

# Evangelism

## Background for the Leader

It is difficult to think about Baptists without thinking about evangelism. Before receiving believer's baptism, a person experiences the transforming power of Jesus Christ and makes a commitment to follow him. With this experience comes joy, forgiveness, liberation, and a new sense of meaning and purpose. Because these new feelings and experiences need to be talked about, there comes a desire to share. But the sharing is also a witness so that others may know this great experience too. That's what evangelism is all about. And that's why evangelism is so basic to being a Baptist.

It is often said that Baptists became a denomination because of mission. Our first national organizational structure, the American Baptist Foreign Mission Society, was formed to support the work of Adoniram and Ann Judson in Burma. The American Baptist Home Mission Society was formed to support mission efforts of people like John Mason Peck on the American frontier. When the Woman's American Baptist Home Mission Society was formed, its first missionary was Joanna P. Moore, already at work among the freed slaves of the American South. It might just as easily be said, however, that Baptists formed denominations because of evangelism, for evangelism was the primary focus of this mission work. The passion to share the Good News with others motivated the Judsons, Peck, Moore, and all those who supported them through the formation of these mission organizations. As Baptists, evangelism has been and still is basic to us.

Just as our understanding of mission has expanded from those early days, so has our understanding of evangelism. In recent years American Baptists have been guided by this definition of evangelism, which was adopted by their General Board in June 1984:

Evangelism is
the joyous witness of the People of God to the redeeming love of God
urging all to repent
and to be reconciled to God and each other
through faith in Jesus Christ who lived, died, and was raised from the dead,
so that
being made new and empowered by the Holy Spirit
believers are incorporated as disciples into the church for worship, fellowship, nurture and engagement in God's mission of evangelism and liberation within society and creation, signifying the Kingdom which is present and yet to come.

That's a pretty inclusive statement. At its core, however, is the sharing of the Good News of Jesus

---

### Biblical Basis
Acts 3:1–16

### Objectives
By the end of the session participants will be able to:
■ describe the work of two Baptist evangelists from our past;
■ identify at least two things they can do to be more effective evangelists;
■ identify at least two things their church does well in the mission of evangelism.

### Key Bible Verse
"I have no silver or gold, but what I have I give you; in the name of Jesus Christ of Nazareth, stand up and walk" (Acts 3:6).

Christ. Despite changes in approach over the years, despite differing styles, that has been and still is what evangelism is all about.

Like mission, our understanding of evangelism needs to be shaped today by the relatively new and all-important reality that the majority of the society in which we live has no ongoing relationship with a church. In the past we had a tendency to think about evangelism as something we do with "them"—people who are different from us. After all, nearly everyone who was like us was already involved in a church! That is no longer the case. This reality calls for an understanding of evangelism that moves beyond the mass event and into personal relationships. A new view of evangelism moves away from a single transforming experience to an ongoing process of being transformed. It calls for *each of us* to develop a renewed commitment to and understanding of the ways in which we are and can be evangelists.

## Exploring the Biblical Basis

Peter was new at the practice we now call evangelism. After all, only a few weeks had passed since Pentecost, when he and others had been sent into the world to share the Good News of Jesus Christ. It must have been a challenge for him to respond correctly, to share appropriately, to help others see the new reality that had so shaped his own life. He might very well have dealt with all the same issues that confront us when it comes to being evangelists.

His interaction with the beggar at the temple, which is the biblical text for this session, was no exception. He was in a new situation that called for a new response. But Peter, led by the Holy Spirit, came through. He responded in a way that enabled faith. In doing so he provided us with a number of important insights about what it means to be an evangelist, insights we can apply to our own lives.

*Peter understood that the gospel comes to people as a response to human need.* The declared need was money. The deeper need was healing. The still deeper need was salvation. It was to the need for healing that Peter responded, even though that wasn't what the man was asking for. It is possible that the man's reason for not asking for healing was a belief that it was impossible.

Perhaps Peter recalled Jesus responding to a crippled man by saying, "Your sins are forgiven" (Mark 2:1–12). But Peter's response was not quite so bold. He chose to meet the man at a level of need that was both real and deep.

*Peter understood what he could offer and what he couldn't.* At least part of Peter's response to the man was based on understanding what he could provide and what he couldn't. Peter offered what he could, and with and through the power of the Holy Spirit, it was enough. Perhaps from the man's perspective it was more than enough. As we share the Good News we must remember that the gospel doesn't solve all problems the way people would like to have them solved. There are some things

we can provide and other things that we must leave to God's infinite wisdom.

*Peter was willing to risk in order to make the Good News real.* The risk for Peter came in at least two ways. First, there was the risk that healing would not come. The claim Peter made was a bold one made in faith. But every act of boldness is a risk. We risk that somehow we may have misread God's intention or misunderstood our purpose. We risk failing to do what we said we would do. In addition to the risk of failure, there was for Peter, and also for us, a second risk, the risk of consequence. The consequence for Peter, within a short period of time, was jail. There are, even in the twenty-first century, consequences when we share the Good News with others.

*Peter was clear about the power behind the Good News.* In conversation with those who witnessed the healing and speeches before his accusers, Peter clearly declared the source of the power that healed. It wasn't him or the act of healing itself that was important; it was the declaration of what that power was. The power of God is what makes healing possible. The power of God is the Good News. Evangelists speak and are empowered by this power.

*Peter understood that all people have complete freedom to respond or not respond to the Good News.* Peter had a clear understanding of his role: it was to bring healing and to explain the source of that healing power. What the beggar, the witnesses, and his accusers did with that was not up to him. It was between them and God.

## As you prepare for this lesson:

**Pray for each participant by name.** We all continually need to be evangelized. We always need to hear Christ's word for us so that we can be brought into closer relationship with God. What word do you need to hear? Think about the members of your class. What might your evangelistic role be with them? Pray that you will know the word that needs to be shared with each of them. Pray also that through this class they may develop a greater sense of themselves as evangelists.

**Read and reflect on the Bible passage** (Acts 3:1–16). If you have time and would like to set these events in the broader context of the days following Pentecost, read Acts 2:1–4:31. Reflect on your own role as an evangelist. Is it one with which you are comfortable? In what ways do you need to grow in that role? Your willingness to share about this with the class members will increase their openness.

**Select an appropriate hymn or praise song to use with the class as a closing.** Several hymns are suggested in Step 6.

## Beginning

**1.** *Do an evangelism pulse check.* *(5–10 minutes)*

■ Welcome class members and explain that this session will explore the importance of evangelism in our Baptist heritage and current mission.

■ Tell the class members that you'd like to begin by taking their "evangelism pulse."

■ Ask them to respond to each of these questions by raising their hands if their answer is yes:

  — Do you think evangelism is important for churches?

  — Are you comfortable sharing about your faith with friends? acquaintances? strangers?

  — Are you an evangelist?

■ Lead a discussion about their responses to these questions, especially those in which there may have been fewer people who responded yes.

■ Use these or your own questions:

  — How is the "evangelism pulse" doing in America? in our community? in our church?

  — Why is evangelism important?

  — How are you an evangelist? How are you not?

## Exploring

**2.** *Respond to a definition of evangelism. (5 minutes)*

■ Distribute handout #9.

■ Ask the class members to look at "Evangelism is . . ."

■ Tell them that this is part of a policy statement on evangelism adopted by the American Baptist Churches, USA in 1984.

■ Write the following key on newsprint or the chalkboard and ask them to use the space on the left to mark each line of the statement:

  **!** if they agree strongly

  **✗** if they disagree

  **?** if they have a question about the meaning of the words

■ Read or ask for a volunteer to read the statement.

■ Review it and discuss the marks class members made.

■ Ask whether they believe any important aspect of evangelism was omitted from the statement.

■ Ask whether thoughts were included that are not part of their understanding of evangelism.

**3.** *Consider biblical insights on evangelism. (10 minutes)*

■ Divide the class into five groups. A group may have only one person in it. Or, if the class is not large enough, do this activity together.

■ Assign one of the five biblical insights on evangelism from the handout to each group.

■ Ask the groups to listen for examples of the insight they have been assigned in the passage you are about to read. They can use the space that is provided to take notes.

■ Read Acts 3:1–16.

■ After you have finished reading the passage, allow about three or four minutes for each group to discuss how they saw the insight illustrated in the passage.

■ Bring the entire group back together and ask each small group to report its findings. Material found in "Exploring the Biblical Basis" will help you supplement this discussion.

**4.** *Explore the lives of two evangelists. (10–15 minutes)*

■ Redivide the class into two groups.

■ Ask one group to read the material on the handout about John Mason Peck, the other about Lulu Fleming, and to look for evidence of the biblical insights in their lives.

■ Allow about five minutes for this work. Then bring the groups back together and ask them to share what they have learned about these two Baptist evangelists.

## Responding

**5.** *Evaluate personal and congregational evangelism. (10–15 minutes)*

■ Ask class members to look once again at "Evangelism is . . ."

and "Biblical Insights on Evangelists."

■ Explain that you would like them to take a few minutes to evaluate both themselves and their church in the mission of evangelism. Put this key on newsprint or the chalkboard:

    **+** for items they/the church do well

    **++** for items they/the church do very well

    **–** for items on which they/the church could improve

    **– –** for items on which they/ the church could improve significantly

■ Reassure class members that the purpose in this is not judgment or criticism, but a desire to improve as evangelists.

■ Allow a few minutes for this work, and then bring the class back together.

■ Ask members to share their insights. Take time to discuss personal concerns as well as actions the church as a whole might take to improve its evangelistic efforts.

■ Explore with class members specific ways in which they can improve. For example, encourage them to talk about specific needs to which they believe they could respond or ways in which they could become more comfortable talking about Christ with others.

**6.** *Close with a song and prayer. (5 minutes)*

■ Briefly review the material you have covered in the session.

■ Point out that you have only scratched the surface on this important topic.

■ Ask whether the discussion has provoked any thoughts or hopes that can be carried further during the coming weeks.

■ Close with a song that affirms the importance of sharing the Good News of Jesus Christ with others. "Pass It On," "Jesus Saves," "People Need the Lord," and "We've a Story to Tell to the Nations" are all possibilities.

■ Close with a prayer thanking God for our Baptist heritage of evangelism and asking for the continuing guidance of God's Spirit as we become better and more effective evangelists.

# CHAPTER 10

# Worship

## Background for the Leader

Ideas about worship abound! There may be as many "Baptist" styles of worship as there are Baptist churches! With no prayer book to guide us, no book of order to govern us, each congregation makes its own decisions about worship. Everything from liturgical formality to charismatic spontaneity happens in Baptist churches. And sometimes both happen in the same Baptist church!

With so many possibilities before us, there is bound to be a healthy disagreement about what is best. There are also, from time to time at least, bound to be outright battles over what happens in the worship service. Even whether or not to sing "Amen" at the end of hymns can be a bone of contention! These disagreements testify to the important role worship plays in our lives. It truly is sacred.

If worship is sacred, it is also in many ways personal. At least that's the way people often approach it. The question many use to evaluate worship is simply, "Was it meaningful to me?" Personal meaning is important, of course, but it is not the whole story. Worship is a corporate experience, something for the people of God gathered together as a community of faith. The "we" of

worship is just as important, if not more important, than the "me" of worship. The focus of worship is God, so rather than "What did I get out of it?" a more appropriate question to ask might be "What did God get out of it?" That question is certainly more difficult to answer, but asking it can, at the very least, help us keep the focus of worship in the right place.

Recent studies of worship and the role it plays in our lives reveal some interesting information. In most churches there seems to be a generational difference in what is seen as "good" worship. One study captured this difference in two simple words. Those born prior to World War II think of worship primarily as *meditation*. Those born following that war think of it primarily as *celebration*. Both are important to worship, but a view of what is *most* important shapes attitudes on a whole array of worship issues. If worship is primarily meditation, a quiet time for personal preparation before worship is essential. But if it is primarily celebration, a joyous time of community sharing makes sense. If worship is meditation, children can be a disruption. But if it is celebration, children help set the proper tone. If worship is meditation, a sermon that prompts personal contemplation is just right.

But if it is celebration, that same sermon can destroy the essential mood. If worship is meditation, prayers of confession play a central role. But if it is celebration, prayers of thanksgiving are most important.

Despite significant personal differences and great differences in worship practices among Baptist churches, there are several important common affirmations we can make. Each of these is related to the heritage we share as Baptists.

**1.** The differences that exist among us result from one of our most basic principles—the autonomy of the local congregation. This is why there is no prayer book, no

---

## Biblical Basis
Psalm 95:1–7a

## Objectives
By the end of the session participants will be able to:
- acknowledge different personal views of what makes worship meaningful;
- name common biblical and Baptist elements of worship.

## Key Bible Verse
"O come, let us worship and bow down, let us kneel before the Lord, our Maker!" (Psalm 95:6).

prescribed form of worship for all to follow.

**2.** The centrality of the Bible in our life and faith is another Baptist principle that shapes our worship. The reading of God's Word and proclamation based on that Word are significant emphases of Baptist worship, even though the style of worship may vary greatly.

**3.** Because we believe in the priesthood of all believers, the proclamation of God's Word deals with living as faithful "priests" in today's world.

**4.** Our understanding of the ordinances of baptism and Communion also provide a common thread for our approach to worship. The similarity in the practice of these two ordinances in Baptist churches is an affirmation of the common heritage we share. The regular gathering at the Lord's Table affirms our unity despite differences. No matter the particular understanding of Communion we bring to that table, we also affirm that Christ is the one who brings us there, and he alone truly unites us.

This session explores worship in Baptist churches. We want not only to celebrate the variety of worship styles among us, but also to affirm the common foundation of praise to God that undergirds all worship.

## Exploring the Biblical Basis

Psalm 95 is one of the most familiar of all the psalms. It is a joyous expression of praise for who God is and what God has done. It expresses in a minimum of words what true worship is all about.

This psalm uses a repeating pattern to call God's people into a worshiping relationship. Verses 1–2 present the invitation: "O come, let us sing to the Lord. . . ." Verses 3–5 remind listeners why this is the right thing to do: "For the Lord is a great God, and a great King above all gods . . . ." That pattern is then repeated. Verse 6 offers the invitation, "O come, let us worship and bow down . . . ," and verse 7 tells us why, "For he is our God. . . ."

Verses 1 and 2 suggest several important elements of our worshiping relationship with God. Singing, joy, thanksgiving, and praise are all parts of worship. The psalm calls us to worship, and worship is doing these things. We are important in worship, it seems to say, because of what we offer to God, not because of what is offered to us.

The reasons for worship provided in verses 3–5 and verse 7 offer another insight. Part of worship is remembering what God has done so that we can know who God is. God has created all things (the depths of the earth, the heights of the mountains, the sea, the dry land). God has cared for us and continues to care (as a shepherd cares for sheep). That is what God has done for us, that is who God is, and that is why we worship God.

Another important insight here is that God is "a great King above all gods." At first that seems like a strange affirmation for a psalm to make. After all, one of the most basic affirmations of our faith is that there is only one God. Why then do we go out of our way to say God is above all other gods? What other gods? This psalm was written in a time of competing gods, each demanding to be the object of worship. Times haven't changed. Back then they called

them gods. Today the issues are more subtle, but many things still compete for our allegiance, things we are tempted to make the object of our living. We place our trust in things, looking to them for security, believing they will offer us purpose and peace. We worship those things instead of God. When we are called to worship, we must remember that God is above all other gods of our own making.

## As you prepare for this lesson:

**Pray for each participant by name.** This session is about encountering the holy in our lives. Because worship is such an important and powerful experience, the topic needs to be approached with an attitude of reverence. As you prepare for this session, offer a prayer for each of the participants as they encounter the "holy" in their lives. Pray for help in developing and leading a session that will enable them to deepen their experience of this encounter in their own lives and together as a worshiping community.

**Read and reflect on the Bible passage** (Psalm 95:1–7a). You might want to use this psalm as the basis for your own devotional experience during the days before the class session. Sometimes familiarity blinds us to the full richness of meaning to be found in a passage. Read this passage over several times slowly. Focus on key words. Find a different translation to read from. As you read the psalm, think about ways the elements of worship that are mentioned happen in your life.

**Select an appropriate hymn or praise song to use with the class**

**as a closing.** Several hymns are suggested in Step 6.

## Beginning

**1.** *Reflect on worship. (5 minutes)*

■ Welcome the class members.

■ Explain that in this session they will be exploring worship: its purpose, what makes it meaningful, and why people have different opinions about it.

■ Announce that to begin the session you will be doing a brief survey about what worship means to them.

■ Explain that you will name two items and would like them to decide which one worship resembles more.

■ Use this example: "I might ask 'For you, is worship more like a towering mountain peak or a lush green valley?' You would then decide which place 'feels' more like worship to you. There are no right or wrong answers. We're just using these as a way to begin to explore some of our own thoughts and feelings about worship."

■ After you give each set of options, ask those who responded each way to raise their hands. Then spend a minute or two talking about the reasons people selected the option they did.

■ Use all of the following options or select the ones that you think will prompt the most discussion in your class. Create some of your own. Make certain, however, to include the last set (celebrating or meditating), as it is referred to in the next step. Worship is more like:

   — a towering mountain peak or a lush green valley

   — a rushing river or a deep ocean

   — a spring evening or an autumn day

   — walking or swimming

   — thinking or feeling

   — celebrating or meditating

■ Ask class members to reflect upon the different opinions about worship that were shared.

■ Have them share other ways in which different opinions about worship are present in your own congregation. It might be that this has been a recent topic of discussion within the church. If so, encourage class members to reflect upon those different opinions and what they have meant for your church.

**2.** *Explore a reason for differences. (5–10 minutes)*

■ Ask class members to recall their responses to the last option you presented to them: worship is more like celebrating or meditating.

■ Explain that one survey of church members showed that those born prior to World War II generally consider worship as meditation, while those born after that war generally consider it celebration. Is this reflected in the way they responded?

■ Distribute handout #10 and ask the class members to turn to "Worship—What Do You Prefer?"

■ Use this material to help the class reflect on ways these two different understandings of worship can influence a worship service.

■ Ask class members if they can think of additional differences these two understandings of worship might make.

■ Ask if either set of answers is really "right."

■ Explore the notion that both sets of options can be meaningful worship and that openness to each preference is a way to broaden our understanding of worship.

■ Use these comments in your own words to bring this step to conclusion: "This helps us understand the important role personal preference plays in our understanding of worship. Personal preference is important because it helps make worship meaningful to us. However, differing personal preferences don't determine whether worship is right or wrong, good or bad. They simply determine what kind of worship each one of us likes. Since the church is made up of people of different ages who have different preferences, worship for everyone should be built on a recognition of these differences."

## Exploring

**3.** *Reflect on Psalm 95. (10–15 minutes)*

■ Point out to the class that you have been focusing on different preferences for worship, but that for the remainder of the session you will be exploring common elements in all styles of worship.

■ Ask class members to turn to "Insights of Psalm 95" on the first page of the handout.

■ Ask them to read the psalm in unison.

■ Use the questions that are included on the handout to help them reflect on the meaning of the psalm. These questions are based in the material found in "Exploring the Biblical Basis." Answers to specific questions may be found there.

■ Next, ask class members to read the quote from Leander Keck that is found in "The Central Focus of Worship."

■ Explain that the "silliness" Keck is concerned about is a focus on worship as a way to meet our needs—on what worship does for us rather than what it does for God. His point is that while there are benefits for us in worship, they are only by-products of worship that is focused on God. When what we get out of worship becomes our primary concern, we lose the legitimate purpose of worship and forfeit the true value it has for us.

■ Offer these two "pictures" of what worship looks like. In the first the pastor, worship leaders, and choir are the "performers," with the congregation as the "audience." In the second, all those gathered to worship (pastor, worship leaders, choir, and congregation) are the "performers" and God is the "audience."

■ Ask which of these pictures supports Keck's view.

■ Discuss which picture more accurately depicts the style of worship expressed in Psalm 95.

**4.** *Share about the "gifts" of worship. (15 minutes)*

■ Ask class members to turn to "The Four Gifts of Worship."

■ Explain that these "gifts" of worship come to us through offering our gift of worship to God. They describe the "by-products" of worship that is truly focused on God.

■ Note also that these gifts are provided for us both in worship that emphasizes celebration and worship that emphasizes meditation. They are another common element of all true worship.

■ If there are more than seven in the class, divide into smaller groups of no more than four. Invite participants to share in their small groups about times in their lives they experienced these gifts of worship. If the class has seven or fewer members, discuss this as a total group.

■ Encourage participants to share their experiences and the reasons they believe the "gifts" were received at those particular times.

■ Bring the class together. Invite the smaller groups to share anything they would like with the entire class.

**5.** *Reflect on "Baptist" worship. (10 minutes)*

■ Review the common elements of worship you have discussed so far: focus on God, offering praise, the gifts of power, community, meaning, and hope.

■ Note that there is yet another common thread you want to explore: the common heritage we share as Baptists and the way it shapes our worship.

■ Ask the class to turn to "What Makes Worship Baptist?" Listed there are a number of commonly assumed Baptist emphases.

■ Ask class members to look at the items on the list and consider ways in which they might provide a common thread for the practice of worship in our Baptist churches.

■ Explain that not all of the emphases may do this, but you want the class to think about which ones might.

■ Discuss the suggestions they make. Also use the material in "Background for the Leader" to point out the relationship between the four Baptist emphases discussed there and our Baptist practice of worship.

## Responding

**6.** *Close with prayer and a song of praise. (5 minutes)*

■ Read or ask a volunteer to read the paragraph about Obadiah Holmes that follows the listing of Baptist emphases.

■ Offer a prayer of thanksgiving to God for the gifts of worship and the ways these have touched and transformed our lives.

■ Close by singing a song of praise such as "O Worship the King," "Praise Him," or "Majesty, Worship His Majesty."

# CHAPTER 11

# Issues of Faith

## Background for the Leader

Christians are called to share God's prophetic word with others. We do this by living out and talking about our faith. We do this as individuals, as churches, and as denominations.

From our earliest days, Baptists have taken stands on issues of faith. Early Baptists learned that taking a stand on issues can be a difficult thing to do. Obadiah Holmes was whipped in Massachusetts for speaking God's word in a worship service held in a friend's home. Other Baptists were ridiculed and jailed for speaking in opposition to state-supported churches. Despite the difficulties, the Baptist tradition of taking a stand continues today in local churches, in regional gatherings, and in national denominational meetings.

This is not an easy thing to do. Sometimes God's word for a particular situation or issue is not clear. Sometimes people of deep faith disagree over what that word might be. Sometimes we do not say anything because we are not clear what word needs to be spoken.

Despite the difficulty and disagreements, Christians are called to speak boldly. Baptist history contains many examples of people who boldly spoke God's word. Isaac Backus spoke boldly for the separation of church and state. Prudence Crandall boldly established a school for African American women in Connecticut before the Civil War. Helen Barrett Montgomery was the first woman member of the Rochester, New York, school board, the first woman president of American Baptists, and a translator of the New Testament in a time when women did not do such things. Edwin Dahlberg boldly spoke against the evil of war. Jennie Clare Adams boldly served in a Philippine hospital and was killed with several other missionaries during World War II. Martin Luther King Jr. spoke eloquently and boldly of a dream he had for all God's people. Individual boldness is not easy. It is a great responsibility. Sometimes it is hard to discern the difference between our opinion and God's word. Sometimes we falsely assume that God has no word to speak because we can't "hear" one. Sometimes, like Jonah, we run and hide.

Our tradition as Baptists inspires and challenges us to speak God's word boldly—even when it is difficult, even when the response may not be positive. As people of faith we have a responsibility to interpret and proclaim, to witness, and to defend the mighty works God is doing in our world.

This session will give you and your class the opportunity to consider ways in which you can remain true to this heritage, both as individuals and as a church.

## Exploring the Biblical Basis

Things were not going well for the disciples. Immediately following Pentecost there had been a great burst of enthusiasm and many converts. It seemed that no power on earth would be able to stop the spread of the Good News.

---

### Biblical Basis
Acts 4:23–31

### Objectives
By the end of the session participants will be able to:
- discuss a biblical rationale for speaking out on important issues;
- become involved in the process of developing a denominational statement.

### Key Bible Verse
"When they had prayed . . . they were all filled with the Holy Spirit and spoke the word of God with boldness" (Acts 4:31).

---

The believers eagerly gathered together to share their meals, to join in prayer, to worship, and to learn from the apostles. When they went out into the world, they couldn't keep silent. Transformed by their new faith, they were compelled to tell others how God's power had made a difference in their lives. That was what got them into trouble.

The trouble began when Peter and John healed a crippled beggar at the temple gate. (See session 9, "Evangelism," for a more detailed study of this story.) Peter made it worse by explaining to the crowd that the power that enabled this healing was the same power that raised the Jesus they had crucified from the dead. Such talk did not sit well with the temple authorities, so they had Peter and John arrested. With a stern warning to never again speak or teach in the name of Jesus, Peter and John were released from prison.

The biblical basis for this session relates the events that occurred immediately following Peter and John's return to the other believers. They told their story; then with the others, they prayed that they might be able to speak God's Word with boldness. The passage reports that their prayer was answered. The room in which they were gathered shook, and they were filled with the Holy Spirit and spoke the word of God.

What would you do if you had been arrested and spent the night in jail? What would you do if you were threatened by the authorities and then released on the condition that you never speak or teach again? What would you do? Like Peter, John, and the other believers,

we might pray. But would our prayers be for boldness? Thanksgiving, perhaps, for our deliverance. Protection, perhaps, so that such a thing would not happen again. But boldness—to speak God's word even more boldly? This is a great prayer indeed!

It always takes boldness to speak God's word. Even though it is a word of salvation based in God's great love for us, it often does not always sit well with those who hear it. Peter learned that early. And anyone who speaks God's word knows that Peter's experience is not unique. Have you known this experience?

Both the Bible and our tradition as Baptists inspire us to speak God's word boldly—even when it is difficult, even when the response may not be a positive one. As people of faith it is our responsibility to interpret and proclaim, to witness and defend the mighty works that God is doing in our world. That's what Peter did, and all those who have followed in his footsteps. It is our heritage and our challenge.

## As you prepare for this lesson:
**Pray for each participant by name.** The value of this session is directly related to the way it speaks to the specific needs and interests of your class members. Pray for them as you prepare. Remember their faces, their lives, and their needs. Ask for God's presence to be with them.

**Read and reflect on the Bible passage** (Acts 4:23–31). For further background on the events described in this passage, read Acts 3:1–4:22. It is a great story, filled with drama

and excitement. Try to become familiar enough with it that you can tell it in your own words for your class.

**Ask someone to share with the class about your denomination's process for resolutions and policy statements.** The conclusion of the session includes time to learn more about the specific process your denomination uses to take stands on issues of faith. If you want to do that, speak with your pastor or someone who knows the process about presenting the information to the class.

**Select an appropriate hymn or praise song to use with the class as a closing.** Several hymns are suggested in Step 6.

## Beginning
**1.** *Share information about Peter. (5 minutes)*
■ Tell the class members that the focus of today's session is "Baptists Take Stands on Issues of Faith."
■ Explain that during the session they will explore some of the various ways Baptists take stands. They will also have an opportunity to look at what some of those issues have been, as well as learn how to contribute to the ongoing discussion of important issues within the denomination.
■ Say something such as: "But first we are going to look at one biblical passage that helps explain why taking a stand on issues of faith is important. It's a story about Peter, so before we begin I'd like us to recall just who Peter was. I'll begin with a simple statement about him. Then someone else in the class can continue by saying, 'Before that, . . .' or 'And then, . . .' followed by

something they know about Peter. We'll continue this way until we've shared what we know about Peter."

■ Begin with this statement: "Peter was one of the first disciples called by Jesus."

■ Encourage class members to continue, reminding them of the two different phrases they can use to introduce what they know about Peter. For example, someone might say, "Before that, he was a fisherman with his brother Andrew."

■ As class members share, write key facts on newsprint or the chalkboard.

■ As this process continues, insure that at least these basic facts about Peter are shared: (1) he was a fisherman; (2) he was one of Jesus' most trusted disciples; (3) following the establishment of the church at Pentecost, he was one of its prominent leaders.

■ Thank the class members for their contributions and invite them to examine an event in Peter's life right after the beginning of the church.

## Exploring

**2.** *Set the scene for Peter.*
*(5–10 minutes)*

■ Tell the class that like all good stories the setting for this one is very important.

■ Explain that you would like them to set the scene for the passage you will be studying by doing a little bit of background research.

■ Divide the class into at least three groups.

■ Indicate that each group's assignment will be to read the passage you give it and then develop a brief description of what the passage says to share with the class.

■ Explain that as they compile these three descriptions, they will be setting the scene for the passage they will all be studying together.

■ Assign one of these passages to each group: Acts 3:1–10; Acts 3:11–26; Acts 4:1–22. If the class has shown a willingness to be creative in the past, you might suggest that they act out these passages. (Note: The basic story line contained in these passages is described in the "Exploring the Biblical Basis" section above.)

■ When all three groups have finished sharing ask: "What would you do now?" If they are slow to answer, remind them of all that Peter has been through and again ask, "What would you do next if all this had happened to you?" Someone may know the story and immediately say, "Pray." Don't let that stop discussion, however.

■ Encourage the class to discuss the possibilities, all the way from going right to the temple to preach and heal again to going back to Galilee to go fishing.

**3.** *Discover what Peter did.*
*(5 minutes)*

■ Invite the class to read Acts 4:23–31 from their Bibles to discover what Peter really did.

■ Ask if they are surprised that Peter went right to the members of his church and prayed with them. Was that one of the responses they had suggested?

■ Ask if they are surprised by what Peter prayed for.

■ Explore the other possible prayer petitions that might have been offered: *protection from the authorities, a change of heart on the part of the authorities, more freedom to speak about Jesus, thanksgiving for being released.*

■ Ask the class members if they would more likely have taken one of these other options.

■ Conclude this step with a statement such as: "In this passage of Scripture, we find Peter taking a stand on the most basic issue of faith. It wasn't an easy stand to take. It led him to prison and incurred the anger of the religious authorities. And yet, Peter did it. More than that, however, he was so convinced of the call to continue to speak God's word that he asked God for even greater boldness. What Peter did here is a model for all of us as people of faith. We, too, are called to speak God's word, even when it is difficult. We, too, need boldness in order to speak as God would have us speak. As Baptists we share a long tradition of speaking God's word on important issues of faith and life."

**4.** *Discuss what issues the church should take a stand on.*
*(10–15 minutes)*

■ Distribute handout #11. Point out "A People Who Speak Out," explaining that you won't be looking at it in class but that it offers background on ways Baptists have taken stands on important issues.

■ Ask class members to look at "Issues for the Church."

■ Read the directions and then allow time for individual work. There may be some frustration at the somewhat artificial distinction between types of issues that is made here. An economic issue may also be a moral issue, as well as a faith issue. If a question is raised about the categories, explain that this is one of the concepts the class will examine next, but that for this step it will help if they can go along with the distinctions that are used on the handout.

■ When class members have finished their individual work, ask them to share their opinions and the reasons for them. Remind them that it is okay if there are significant differences of opinion.

■ After allowing several minutes for this discussion, ask class members about their decision-making process: How did they decide what issues the church should speak out on? Was it easy for them to decide or difficult? Was there agreement or disagreement among class members on the type of issues the church should speak about? Which of these do they believe are "faith issues"?

■ This discussion may bring up areas of struggle or disagreement among class members. If it does, suggest that this is one of the reasons it is difficult for denominations to take a stand on important issues, but that the difficulty involved does not excuse us from trying to reach consensus.

**5.** *Discuss what the church should say about an issue. (10–15 minutes)*

■ Move the discussion further along by selecting one of the issues from the list on the handout and asking class members what they believe the church should say about it. You might want to select an issue on which you know there is some difference of opinion. The purpose of this discussion is to point out that an additional difficulty in speaking out is that people of deep faith often disagree about what God wants them to say.

■ Avoid getting into a great debate; simply have members state their opinions.

■ If there is agreement among class members, you can introduce the notion of differing opinions by asking if they think all Baptists would agree with their position, or if those who live in a different place or have a different theological perspective might view the issue differently.

## Responding

**6.** *Explore ways of speaking out. (5 minutes)*

■ Share with the class that despite difficulties, Baptists share the conviction that it is important to speak out on issues of importance to our faith and world. In this we follow a tradition that goes back even beyond Peter to the prophets of the Old Testament.

■ Explore with the class their interest in learning more about resolutions and policy statements that your denomination develops. If there is interest in pursuing this, speak with your pastor about the process for formulating denominational resolutions and statements. If you have asked your pastor or someone else to share with the class about this process, ask him or her to do that now.

**7.** *Close with a song and prayer. (5 minutes)*

■ Close with a prayer asking that we, like Peter, might be bold enough to speak God's word even in the face of difficulty.

■ If the class enjoys singing, close with an appropriate hymn, such as: "Lord, Speak to Me That I May Speak," "Open My Eyes, That I May See," and "God of Grace and God of Glory."

# CHAPTER 12

# Prophetic Role

## Background for the Leader

Christians face a great challenge today—living in a non-Christian world. How do we speak and act as disciples in a culture that is in many ways alien to the gospel? This is a prophetic challenge that involves speaking and living out God's Word so that the world sees, hears, and understands the gospel. Baptists have a long tradition of speaking a prophetic word even when it goes against societal norms. We began by challenging government interference in personal faith, and we continue to apply the gospel to societal issues. In this session we will look at ways Baptists, both as individuals and with others, have played this prophetic role of bringing God's Word to the world.

Baptists were born a prophetic people. From the very beginning they brought God's Word to bear on the significant issues of life. Baptists began as a people of protest; they stood against the usual and customary ways of thinking and acting. When others believed a civil society was impossible without a state religion, Baptists founded a colony that granted full liberty of conscience in matters of religion. Roger Williams in Providence and John Clarke in Newport were prophets of a new way to understand relationships between the state and the church. This prophetic call was taken up in later times by John Leland in Virginia and Isaac Backus in Massachusetts. It continues to be a Baptist witness today.

While religious freedom was our first, and perhaps greatest, prophetic witness, it is not our only one. Baptists stood tall against the evil of slavery, even though it meant the division of our historic mission societies. Baptists have been prophets of peace in the midst of violence, prophets of justice in the midst of oppression, and prophets of hope in the midst of despair and destruction. Charles Evans Hughes, as secretary of state, and Edwin Dahlberg, as a pastor, were prophets of peace in the world. Isabel Crawford, as a missionary to the Kiowas, and Walter Rauschenbusch, as a seminary professor and author, were prophets of social justice. Betty Miller and Jitsuo Morikawa, as denominational leaders, proclaimed a prophetic message about what it meant to live as people who share the Christian faith in the mid-twentieth century. Baptists today continue to proclaim a prophetic message about what it means at the beginning of the twenty-first century to live as people who share the Christian faith.

The prophet's role is not an easy one. It is difficult for the individual, perhaps even more so for a denomination. First, it is a matter of seeking God's word, of discovering what God is saying in a particular time and place about a particular situation or issue. Even if one person has a strong sense of this word, there is still the need to have it tested within the community of faith. For a denomination the process of developing a sense of God's word in the midst of often opposing views is arduous and

---

### Biblical Basis
1 Peter 2:1–12

### Objectives
By the end of the session participants will be able to:
- describe the prophetic ways of three Baptists;
- name specific steps they can take to be prophets today.

### Key Bible Verse
"You are a chosen race, a royal priesthood, a holy nation, God's own people, in order that you may proclaim the mighty acts of him who called you out of darkness into his marvelous light" (1 Peter 2:9).

seemingly impossible. If the word becomes clear, if it is sustained in testing, there still remains the challenge of speaking it clearly and of living it. All of this can drain the spirit of even the most faithful among us.

Despite the difficulties, Baptists continued to assume the prophetic role that comes with being God's people. This is our heritage, a heritage that both challenges and inspires us as we live in a world that continues so often to be at odds with the Good News.

## Exploring the Biblical Basis

Early Christians knew what it was like to live in a world that was alien to the gospel, a world in which only a minority professed, shared, and lived by the Christian faith. Living a Christian life put them at odds with all other major religions of the day. Even Judaism, the faith from which they grew, offered hostile opposition to their existence. Yet the Christians continued to proclaim God's Word, to share God's love, and to grow as churches. It wasn't easy. The First Letter of Peter was written to these early Christians in the midst of their struggle and persecution. It offers both encouragement and challenge. In the words of *The New Interpreter's Bible*, ". . . the epistle helps to strengthen Christians in times of distress; sets their lives within the history of God's activity, which moves from creation to consummation; holds up the atoning death of Jesus Christ; and encourages mutual love among Christian people and forbearance of enemies."[1] Peter describes the reality early Christians

faced and calls the early followers of Christ to faithfulness.

The passage that is our focus in this session spans two sections of Peter's letter. Verses 1–10 conclude a section that describes God's holy people. Verses 11–12 begin a section on what it means for Christians to live in an alien world of nonbelievers. Thus, we see in it both an affirming description of the faithful and an inspiring challenge to faithful living. This challenge is a call to speak and live a prophetic word.

The passage begins by listing the negative qualities Christians should set aside and describing what they should seek in their lives. Malice, guile, insincerity, envy, and slander are destructive to the community and make growing in faith impossible. They can be countered, much as a mother's milk protects a baby from infection, by "pure, spiritual milk" that enables growth in salvation.

Verses 4 through 8 use the image of "living stones" being "built into a spiritual house" to affirm a close relationship between God's work in Christ and in them. Peter reminds his readers of the ease with which the world rejects the faith, and he encourages them to remain faithful despite rejection. Believers can do this by offering "spiritual sacrifices acceptable to God" and remaining obedient to God's Word.

Verse 9, which is the key verse for this session, boldly affirms who Christians are and what they are to do. Christians are "a chosen race, a royal priesthood, a holy nation, God's own people" so that they might "proclaim the mighty acts" of God. This purpose goes beyond their own salvation; they are called to play a prophetic role for God.

God's mighty acts are not simply what God has done in Jesus Christ, as wondrous as that is. They also include God's continuing work in the world—calling them and us "out of darkness into his marvelous light." That work carries on as others are called to the light, as God's love is shared, as God's kingdom comes. This is a biblical warrant for our lives as a prophetic people.

Attempts to respond to God's prophetic call often become divisive within churches and denominations. This passage makes an important affirmation that helps us deal with this reality. It is a theme that runs throughout these verses but is most clearly stated at the beginning: "Rid yourselves, therefore, of all malice, and all guile, insincerity, envy, and all slander." These are words about the way in which members of the Christian community are to treat each other. This theme is picked up again in verses 11 and 12. The "desires of the flesh" are not limited to those of a sensual nature. They include all sins that spring from a focus on self, turning one away from others and from God. This self-centered behavior is precisely that which the author encourages us to set aside in verse 1. The reason for this is clearly stated in verse 12: More than a matter of personal purity, it is so nonbelievers "may see your honorable deeds and glorify God when he comes to judge." The way we treat one another is one of our greatest witnesses to the power of God's love. It is one of the clearest prophetic words we can speak in a world in which love is so often lacking in relationships, especially among those who disagree with one another.

## As you prepare for this lesson:

**Pray for your participants by name.** Many of those participating in the class likely come from non-Baptist backgrounds. This class will help them learn more about the denomination of which they have become a part. Some may be active and vocal in proclaiming what they believe to be a prophetic word in your church and your community. Others may not have given much thought at all to the prophetic call that comes to all Christians. As you prepare, pray that class members will be open to one another and to the Word of God.

**Read and reflect on the session's Bible passage** (1 Peter 2:1–12). Although 1 Peter is less well known than some of the other New Testament epistles, many will be familiar with the passage that is the basis for this session. Its dramatic imagery makes it perhaps the best-known passage in 1 Peter. The letter itself is not long, so you may want to read it in its entirety. If that is not possible, take time to read 2:1–12 and "Exploring the Biblical Basis." This will provide essential information for your teaching.

**Write the statement about prophets on chalkboard or newsprint.** This description is found in Step 1.

**Select an appropriate hymn or praise song to use with the class as a closing.** Several hymns are suggested in Step 6.

## Beginning

**1.** *List prophets of note.*
*(5–10 minutes)*
■ Welcome class members.
■ Talk briefly with them about events of the past week, both in their lives and in the world.

■ Write the word *Prophets* on the chalkboard or newsprint.
■ Ask class members to name people who were or are prophets. As the list develops, encourage the class to include biblical, historical, and contemporary prophets.
■ Ask, "What makes a prophet a prophet?"
■ Discuss answers that class members give.
■ Following this discussion, share this description, which you have written on the chalkboard or newsprint: *A prophet is a person who speaks or acts out God's Word for a particular people, time, and place.*
■ Explain that the key ability of the prophet is to discern the way God is at work in the world and to share that with others.
■ Point out that this can be related either to a personal issue in someone's life or to important social and/or political issues.
■ Ask if there is a prophet speaking to any of the events they talked about at the beginning of this session.
■ Briefly discuss their responses.

## Exploring

**2.** *Learn about Baptist prophets.*
*(20 minutes)*
■ Distribute handout #12.
■ Divide the class into three groups and explain that you will be taking some time now to look at the lives of three Baptists who spoke and lived a prophetic word in their time.
■ Assign one person described in "Three Baptist Prophets" to each group.
■ Allow time for each group to read about the person and discuss his or her importance as a prophet.

■ Ask the groups to prepare a brief presentation for the entire class.
■ Encourage them to be creative in these presentations; suggest these possibilities: A group might find a volunteer to role-play the prophet and the others in the group could interview him or her. A group might develop a "key facts" sheet about the person and print it on newsprint for the entire class to see. Or a group might produce a news report about one significant event in the prophet's life and add other information as background.
■ Allow about 10 minutes for preparation, and then have each group share its work with the class.
■ Ask:
  — What similarities did these three prophets share?
  — What differences could be found in their lives?
  — What do these similarities and differences tell us about what it means to be a prophet?

**3.** *Study 1 Peter 2:1–12.*
*(10–15 minutes)*
■ Remind the class that these three presentations illustrate our Baptist heritage as a people who are willing to seek, speak, and act God's Word.
■ Note that the foundation for this heritage is in the Bible itself.
■ Ask the class to turn to 1 Peter 2:1–12 in their Bibles.
■ Use the material in the first two paragraphs of "Exploring the Biblical Basis" to introduce this passage and explain its relevance to today's theme.
■ Read or ask someone in the class to read the passage.
■ Use the questions in "Exploring God's Prophetic Word" on the handout to guide a discussion.

- Tell the class that all of these questions ask for opinions; there are no right or wrong answers. They are intended to provoke discussion and enable the class to experience some of what is involved in seeking and speaking God's Word.

**4.** *Discuss guidelines for a Christian community. (5 minutes)*
- Read or summarize the material in the last paragraph of "Exploring the Biblical Basis" to introduce this step.
- If your discussion in the previous step revealed a difference of opinion, use that as an example of how our prophetic role often involves controversy.
- Ask the group to identify recent controversies in churches and denominations.
- Ask:
  — What attempts to seek and speak a prophetic word have you witnessed that may have caused these controversies?
  — What insights in this passage might be helpful?
  — What guidelines do these verses offer for churches and denominations that may experience controversy in determining God's prophetic word for today?

## Responding

**5.** *Consider next steps. (5–10 minutes)*
- Ask the class: "On a scale of one to ten, with ten being the best, how would you rate yourself as one who seeks, speaks, and acts a prophetic word?" (This might also be done by establishing an imaginary continuum in the room, with one wall representing a one and the opposite wall a ten. Invite class members to move to the spot on the continuum that represents their answer.)
- Allow time for discussion.
- Ask: "On a scale of one to ten, with ten being the best, how would you rate our church as one that seeks, speaks, and acts a prophetic word?"
- Again, allow time for discussion.
- Ask: "Do your responses to these questions suggest a need for change? If so, what step(s) might be taken as individuals and as a church to follow more fully in this aspect of our Baptist heritage?"
- List all suggestions on the chalkboard or newsprint.
- Give class members each an index card. Ask them to write on one side something from the list they would be willing to do individually and on the other side something they would like the church to do.

**6.** *Close with a song and prayer. (5 minutes)*
- Review the session using words such as these: "Today we've looked at our Baptist heritage as prophets—people willing to seek, speak, and act a prophetic word. We've seen how that role has its foundation in the Bible. We looked at three Baptists who put this belief into action in their own lives. And finally, we've considered what all of this means for us, both as individuals and as a church."
- Ask those who are willing to share an item from their index card as a prayer request.
- Invite the class to join in singing a hymn that deals with this theme, such as "O Young and Fearless Prophet," or "God of Grace and God of Glory."
- Close with prayer lifting up the prayer requests, thanking God for the heritage we share as people of faith and as Baptists, and asking God for the wisdom and strength to remain faithful to that heritage.

## Note
1. David L. Bartlett, "1 Peter," *The New Interpreter's Bible* (Nashville: Abingdon, 1998), 12:233.

# CHAPTER 13

# Diversity

## Background for the Leader

Diversity is and always has been a reality. People are different—in dress, values, skin color, and language. Even Christians have differences. We have a variety of ideas about what meaningful worship is and about the church and its purpose. Every day we are confronted by the differences that abound in the world and are thus challenged to search for common bonds that bring us together. When we find common bonds, it becomes easier for us to affirm our differences rather than fear them. This is true in society. It is also true in the church. Just as there is diversity within churches of different denominations, there is diversity among Baptist churches as well. The purpose of this session is to discover some of the differences that exist and to affirm the common bonds that hold us together. In this way our differences can be seen more clearly as a source of strength and a reason for celebration.

In the United States racial/ethnic diversity is increasing along with the awareness that diversity exists. The Asian and Hispanic populations of the United States have seen significant growth in recent years, and African Americans and Native Americans play a more significant role in the discussion of what and who our nation is than they did even in the recent past. These factors have a significant impact on all of us. They make us aware of change and of the fact that change is often difficult to manage. They cause us to wonder what common bonds unite us when the common values, color, and heritage that once held communities together no longer work. They create fear because differences make it more difficult to understand, to communicate, to care.

The other side to this coin of diversity is that as it grows and we become more aware of it, we open ourselves to the possibility of being enriched by the experience and gifts of others. Whether it be something as simple as food or as complex as an understanding of relationships, diversity offers to us the opportunity to learn from each other and grow together.

What is true culturally is also true denominationally. Most Baptist denominations are becoming more diverse. Once predominantly white, American Baptist Churches in the U.S.A. may soon be a denomination in which no racial/ethnic group has majority status. Statistics can't tell the whole story, but they do help us begin to see the picture of a new and growing reality. In 1995 resident membership of American Baptist churches was 53 percent Euro-American, 42 percent African American, 3 percent Hispanic, 1 percent Asian, and .1 percent Native American. Recent years demonstrate a clear trend of a decline in Euro-American members and an increase in all others.[1] This diversity is both a reason for great celebration and a great challenge.

---

### Biblical Basis
Acts 10:34–35;
Galatians 3:26–29

### Objectives
By the end of the session participants will be able to:
■ affirm the difficulties and benefits of diversity within their congregation;
■ describe the historic and current basis for unity within the diversity of Baptist denominations.

### Key Bible Verse:
"So there is no difference between Jews and Gentiles, between slaves and free men, between men and women: you are all one in union with Christ Jesus" (Galatians 3:28, TEV).

---

We celebrate the fact that Baptist roots are deeply set in different racial/ethnic communities. All in their own way have found something in being Baptist that enables an important expression of who they are and who they believe God is. We celebrate the fact that Baptists, for a number of reasons but largely because of our historic emphasis on local church autonomy, have long been a diverse group of people. Significant differences have always existed among us, but we still have found ways to be together. We celebrate the richness of our diverse heritage that enables us to enrich our own faith through interaction with and learning from others. We celebrate the great opportunity we have as Baptists to work out our relationships in a context of diversity and recognize that as we do so within the church, we enable it to happen within society.

One challenge we face is to change old patterns in order to enable new relationships. Another is to continue to affirm the common bonds that unite us even amid great differences. As Christians we must grow together as a whole people of God and not become isolated pockets of homogeneity. We can begin to meet these challenges by becoming more aware and more affirming of the diversity that exists in our own congregations, whether racial/ethnic diversity or diversity of another kind, such as in worship or music styles, theology, age groupings, or something as basic as a difference of opinion about the proper dress for worship. Any diversity calls us as God's people and as Baptists to seek the common bonds that unite us despite our differences and asks

us to find an openness to one another that enables us to affirm and learn from our differences.

## Exploring the Biblical Basis

In this session we turn to Peter and Paul to discover how they handled the issue of diversity within the early church.

The background for Peter's affirmation of Acts 10:34–35 is found in the story that begins with Acts 10:1. Cornelius was a Roman centurion stationed in Caesarea, the Roman headquarters in Palestine. He had shown interest in the Jewish religion and probably had adopted many of their practices, although he had not converted to Judaism. One afternoon he had a vision in which he clearly saw an angel of God and heard the angel direct him to make contact with Peter. He immediately sent his servants in search of Peter. The next day Peter had a vision; this one was a bit more difficult to interpret. While resting on the roof of the house where he was staying, Peter saw what appeared to be a large sheet descending from heaven. In it were a variety of animals that Jews, according to their dietary laws, were not allowed to eat. A voice commanded, "Get up, Peter; kill and eat." Peter protested, knowing that it was against the Jewish law, but the voice continued until the sheet was taken back up into heaven. While Peter pondered the meaning of this vision, word came of the arrival of Cornelius's servants. After hearing their story, Peter went with them to Caesarea, where Cornelius warmly greeted him and described his vision. Peter's

reply begins in Acts 10:34–35: "I now realize that it is true that God treats all men alike. Whoever fears him and does what is right is acceptable to him, no matter what race he belongs to" (TEV). The vision was a call to Peter to move beyond the common bond of the law to a new common bond, faith in Christ; to embrace a new diversity of race among God's people.

Paul also dealt with the issue of diversity within the early church. He was the strongest advocate of the mission to the Gentiles. Paul did all he could to incorporate them into the body of Christ without imposing the Jewish law upon them. For Paul, too, there was to be a new common bond, faith in Christ. In the letter to the Galatians, Paul was writing to a church that upset him by listening to a group that claimed followers of Christ must also observe the Jewish law. Throughout the letter he is strong in his condemnation of this view. Repeatedly, Paul sounds the theme of unity in Christ despite social or cultural differences. His strongest affirmation of this view is our passage: "So there is no difference between Jews and Gentiles, between slaves and free men, between men and women; you are all one in union with Christ Jesus" Galatians 3:28 (TEV). In Christ the old distinctions do not disappear; they just don't count for anything anymore. One is still Jew or Greek, slave or free, man or woman, but it doesn't make any difference in the eyes of God or in the eyes of believers. Being together in Christ is such a strong bond of unity that all differences become irrelevant. This becomes the standard by which Christians treat each other.

## As you prepare for this lesson:

**Pray for each participant by name.**
This session is about people who are different from us. Differences often prompt interest, but they can also provoke fear. What is different we often do not understand; what we do not understand we often fear. In that fear lies a tendency to view those who are different as wrong or perhaps even as a threat. And yet God created the world full of differences, so that we might enjoy them and our lives might be enriched by them. Knowing this encourages us to be open to different people, ways, and ideas, even if we may not understand them. Be aware of this tension between fear and openness in yourself and your students as you prepare for this session. Offer a prayer for each of the participants as he or she deals with diversity. Pray for help to develop and lead a session that will enable the participants to deepen their appreciation of diversity in their lives, in their community, and in their church.

**Read and reflect on the Bible passages** (Acts 10:34–35; Galatians 3:26–29). Read both passages that are the Bible basis for this session. Reading Acts 10:1–11:18 will give you the full story of Peter and Cornelius and the important role their relationship played in enabling diversity within the early church. If you have time, read the entire Letter to the Galatians. It is only six chapters and provides a wonderful affirmation of the common bond Christians share in Christ, along with stern warnings about falling away from Christ.

**Select an appropriate song to use in the closing.** Several suggestions are made in Step 6.

## Beginning

**1.** *Share differences with the class.*
*(5 minutes)*
■ Welcome class members and let them know that this session will have a special focus on diversity among Baptists.
■ Tell the class that before you look at the "big picture" of diversity in the denomination you want to look at the "little picture" of diversity in the class.
■ Go around the group, asking each class member to complete this sentence: "I am different from others in this class because . . . ."
■ Explain that the difference can be anything: age, looks, interests, beliefs, or something else.
■ After everyone has had a chance to share, ask, "If we're so different, why are we here together?"
■ Take a minute or two to explore their responses, listing them on newsprint or the chalkboard.

**2.** *Share differences within the church and denomination.*
*(5 minutes)*
■ Tell the class you would like to begin to broaden the picture by looking at differences within your church.
■ Ask class members to name ways in which people in the congregation are different. As they do, list the differences on another sheet of newsprint or in a new column on the chalkboard. Differences might include age, race, the kind of church music people like, the type of worship experience that is meaningful to them, or the version of the Bible people like. Perhaps there has been an issue of discussion or even controversy in the church recently. That, too, would be a point of difference, so include it on your list.

■ Next, tell the class you would like to broaden the picture even further by looking at differences that exist among Baptist churches in your association, area, region, and country. If some in the class are active in the wider life of your denomination, their insights would be particularly helpful here. Others can share impressions of differences they have formed based on their attendance at events or on articles they've read in regional or denominational publications. List these differences on a third sheet of newsprint or in a third column on the chalkboard.
■ Invite the class to look at the three lists they have created.
■ Then ask: "If we are so different, what is it that brings us together, that makes us all Baptists?"
■ Record the responses, but avoid a lengthy discussion at this time. Help the class to see that one of the reasons they are together is that although they have differences, they also have things in common that provide a bond.

## Exploring

**3.** *Explore the Bible passages.*
*(20 minutes)*
■ Explain that the early church also had to deal with the issue of diversity; it was probably the most important and difficult issue they faced.
■ Tell the class that they are going to explore how the two major leaders of the early church, Peter and Paul, dealt with the issue of diversity in their ministry.
■ Distribute handout #13.
■ Divide the class into two groups. Ask them to turn to "Peter and Paul Respond to Diversity" on the handout. Ask one group to read

the material and follow the directions in "Peter and a Vision." Ask the other group to do the same for "Paul and the Law."
■ Allow about 10 minutes for the two groups to do their work, and then bring the class back together so each group can report on its discoveries.

4. *Explore a basis for unity as Baptists. (15 minutes)*
■ Ask the class to turn to the statistics in their handout that describe the makeup of one Baptist denomination, the American Baptist Churches.
■ Discuss their reaction to these figures. Ask:
— Do the numbers surprise you?
— In what ways are these patterns similar to our denomination? our congregation?
— What challenges does this present to us?
■ Refer back to the sharing that was done in the last step, noting that Christ is the most important common bond we share, the most important source of unity in the midst of the growing diversity of Baptists.

■ Explain that important parts of our Baptist heritage both explain the diversity that exists and provide a basis for unity in the midst of it.
■ Ask class members to turn to "Baptist Principles." Read the material together.
■ Ask the class in what ways these two principles both explain and help us deal with growing diversity.

## Responding

5. *Determine ways to affirm and celebrate diversity. (10 minutes)*
■ Invite the class to review the discussion of this session, with particular attention to the points of diversity that have been considered.
■ Ask whether there is one point that is of particular concern to them, personally, one that they would like to make a particular effort to affirm and celebrate. Perhaps it is a difference that exists within their own church; perhaps it is a difference between their church and another nearby church.
■ Encourage the class to make plans to contact those involved in the differences they named

and to develop a means of sharing with each other about it so that the differences can be affirmed and celebrated. Consider ways in which both biblical and Baptist principles apply.

6. *Close with an affirmation of unity in Christ. (5 minutes)*
■ Ask the class to join in singing a song that affirms our unity in Christ. "The Bond of Love," "Bind Us Together, Lord," "In Christ There Is No East or West," and "The Church's One Foundation" are all possibilities.
■ Close with a prayer of thanksgiving for the diversity that exists among us as Baptists and for the common bonds, especially the bond of Christ, that hold us together.

## Note
1. Percentages prepared by David Cushman based on the 1995 Annual Reports of the ABC/USA by using simple linear regression with about twenty years of figures from the Congregational Profile System database.

# CHAPTER 14

# Mission

## Background for the Leader

Baptists are a mission people: they desire to engage in mission. The realization that the task was too great for any single church led to the beginnings of Baptist denominational life. Churches united, and together they formed the foreign and home mission societies. They worked to publish resources to distribute and to reach people for Christ. This zeal for mission continues. Mission is more than just what national and regional organizations do, however. Because many people do not attend church, America is one of the world's greatest mission fields. Increasingly, the local congregation is seen as a mission outpost.

At one time mission was something that happened "out there"— in the place to which we sent missionaries. We gave our financial support so missionaries could be sent. We listened to the verbal and written reports of the great work made possible because of our giving. But most of the time we had little direct involvement in mission ourselves. "Out there" might be in Africa or Asia, or any foreign land, among people who had not had the opportunity we had to learn about Christ. Or, it might be here in our own country among people who were seen as "needy." Most often,

however, we didn't think about mission as happening in our own communities, in our own churches, through our Sunday school and our worship service.

All that has changed. Mission still happens "out there," but now it is clear that it happens, it must happen, "right here," too. We live in an unchurched society. More than half of our fellow citizens have no significant relationship to a church. Our friends and neighbors, just as much as those halfway around the world, are in need of Christian missionary presence in their lives so they can come to know the saving grace of Jesus Christ.

This means that our understanding of mission—where it happens, how it happens, and who does it— is expanding. Baptist national and regional mission agencies are still vitally important in our worldwide mission effort. They do things no single church could ever accomplish on its own. But now the mission work of the local congregation has taken on new meaning. Virtually every church is a mission outpost in its community, seeking to be a Christian presence in a culture and society that does not know, but needs to know, the Good News.

This expanded understanding of mission has many implications. Denominational structures were

created to support mission "out there." Now, structure is needed, both within the denomination and the congregation, to ensure that mission happens "right here" as well. Mission giving used to be something separate from the local budget of the church. Now that distinction is no longer as clear. Money used to support the congregation is as much mission giving as is money sent to support a missionary in another country. Both are important. Both are essential. But this is a different way to think about it.

Mission has always been a driving force in Baptist life. Adoniram

### Biblical Basis
Acts 1:6–11

### Objectives
By the end of the session participants will be able to:
- describe several mission efforts of Baptists;
- discuss new mission possibilities for their own church.

### Key Bible Verse
"You will be my witnesses in Jerusalem, in all Judea and Samaria, and to the ends of the earth" (Acts 1:8).

Judson, the first Baptist missionary from America, was halfway to India before Bible study led him to a belief in believer's baptism. Once Baptists in the United States learned they already had a Baptist missionary on the field, they embraced Judson and his passion for mission. Soon the American Baptist Foreign Mission Society was formed in 1814 to support his work. Similar passion led to the development of the Home Mission Society in 1832. Reaching people for Christ also happens through the printed word and through education. So a passion for mission led to the founding of the American Baptist Publication Society, another mission organization. Over the years, as regional groupings of churches in associations and state conventions developed, a passion for mission led them into important work within their own areas. This same passion for mission is at work in new ways today, with a special focus on the local congregation. Baptists are a missionary people. We always have been, and by God's grace, we always will be.

## Exploring the Biblical Basis

The disciples were playing a waiting game. Ever since the amazing day on which Jesus rose from the dead, they had waited—waited for Jesus to appear to them again, waited for the promised coming of God's Spirit. Jesus did come. One last time. They knew it was a special time, and so they asked the question that had been on their minds for days now. "Is this the time you will restore the kingdom to Israel?" In other words, "Is this the time

you will make it the way it used to be for us?" Jesus answered by telling them not to worry about time schedules— this was God's concern, not theirs. But then he went on, telling them what they should be doing until God's time was fulfilled. "You will be my witnesses," he said, "in Jerusalem, in all Judea and Samaria, and to the ends of the earth." To paraphrase, "You will be the ones who tell the world about God's work and love, about the great things God has done and continues to do, about the promise God made that can now be claimed by everyone. You will witness to all of that in what you say and in what you do everywhere you go."

Then, ascending into heaven, Jesus left them. And there they stood gazing after him until two messengers from God came along and said, "What are you doing standing here? There's work to be done!"

In this day when the whole notion of what mission is, and how and where it happens is being reconsidered, these words of Jesus are especially important for us. Like the disciples, we too, may be longing for past greatness—the way things used to be. But Jesus ignores our concern, not out of callousness, but because he knows there is something more important for us to be about. Instead, he directs our attention to the task at hand—being his witnesses. We start where we are. For the disciples it was Jerusalem; for us it may well be our own community. From there we go where Jesus points the way: to Judea, the surrounding countryside; to Samaria, the neighboring, yet alien and somewhat hostile territory; and

on to the ends of the earth. Like the disciples, we may hear these words and be overwhelmed, so much so that we just stand there. We plan but don't move. We talk but don't act. We gaze into the skies wondering what possible difference we can make. But for us, too, there must come the time when we hear the words, perhaps spoken by another, perhaps spoken within our own hearts, "What are you doing standing here? There's work to be done!"

## As you prepare for this lesson:
**Pray for each participant by name.** This session is about putting our faith into action by becoming involved in mission. It encourages us to move beyond words to actions—both in supporting the mission that is done on our behalf by others and through our own personal involvement. As you think about the members of your class, pray for the mission involvement they already have. They are witnesses for Christ in the different arenas of their lives. Give thanks to God for this mission. Pray that you and they will be open to hearing God's encouraging word during this class session. Pray that you might be led into fuller participation in God's mission in the world.

**Learn about and pray for the mission of Baptists.** Our Baptist mission is spread throughout the world, from the work of local congregations to that of missionaries in far-off lands who are supported by denominational structures, and even further to the cooperative work of the Baptist World Alliance.

**Read and reflect on the Bible passage** (Acts 1:6–11). Read the

Bible passage you will be studying. Reflect on the places that are comparable to Jerusalem, Judea, and Samaria in your life and the lives of your students. Think about the ways people are and can be witnesses for Christ.

**Select an appropriate song to use in the closing.** Several suggestions are made in Step 7.

## Beginning

**1.** *Explore views of mission. (5 minutes)*

■ Welcome class members and explain that today you will be exploring the many ways Baptists support and are involved in mission.

■ Write the word *Mission* on newsprint or the chalkboard.

■ Ask the class members to brainstorm words that come to mind when they hear that word.

■ Write their responses. If they need some prompting, suggest that they begin by answering these questions about mission: What is it? Where does it happen? Who does it?

■ When the brainstorming is completed, invite the class to reflect on the words you have listed. Ask: "What conclusions can you draw about the view of mission that you shared?"

## Exploring

**2.** *Explore the new age of mission. (5 minutes)*

■ Distribute handout #14 and ask class members to look at "A New Age of Mission." This is a condensation of material found in "Background for the Leader," so you may want to draw on that section of the

leader's guide for additional insights during this discussion.

■ Ask a volunteer to read the first two paragraphs. These describe an older view of mission as exclusively "out there," and a newer view that sees mission happening "right here" as well.

■ Ask class members for their reactions to the reading. Questions that might help spark discussion include:

— Does the significant number of people who are not actively involved in a church make America a mission field?

— What kind of mission activity do you think would be most effective in the U.S.?

**3.** *Look at a biblical foundation for mission. (5–10 minutes)*

■ Ask class members to open their Bibles to Acts 1:6–11. Set the scene for the passage by explaining that this event occurs at the end of Jesus' time on earth, following the resurrection. Luke has described the event briefly at the conclusion of his gospel, but now comes back to it at the beginning of Acts. He does that because through these words Jesus provides a missionary charge to the church.

■ Ask someone to read the passage aloud.

■ Ask for ideas on the meaning of the word *witness*.

■ Point out the outward movement of Jesus' missionary charge: Jerusalem, Judea, Samaria, to the ends of the earth.

■ Ask the class what places might be named if Jesus were speaking to us about mission today.

■ Point out the response of the disciples to Jesus' charge: they simply remain where they are, gazing up into heaven, until two men arrive

and ask them why they are just standing there.

■ Ask the class in what ways, if any, this image might describe a typical reaction of the church (the church in general, not necessarily their local church specifically) to Jesus' missionary challenge.

**4.** *Learn about two mission outposts. (10 minutes)*

■ Tell the class that as Baptists we have traditionally taken this missionary charge very seriously; the roots of our denomination are found in the need to send missionaries—something no one local church could do alone.

■ Explain that in order to get a quick picture of ways in which this charge is carried out today, they will be learning about two different mission outposts supported by Baptists.

■ Ask them to turn to "Baptist Mission Outposts" on the handout.

■ Divide the class into two groups. Ask each group to read one of the stories and prepare to present it to the rest of the class.

■ Allow several minutes for the groups to do their reading, then bring the class back together so the groups can present the stories to each other.

■ When both groups have shared, ask these questions:

— What about these places makes what they do mission?

— What needs of the people are being met by the missionaries?

— How are the missionaries being witnesses for Jesus Christ?

**5.** *Consider your church as a mission outpost. (10–15 minutes)*

■ Point out that these two stories describe being witnesses in places that might be the "Judea" and "Samaria" that Jesus talked about.

■ Tell the class that now you want them to turn their attention to "Jerusalem," their own community.

■ Ask: "In what ways do you think your church is a mission outpost?"

■ To help the class members consider this question, ask them to quickly brainstorm all the activities of your church, from worship to the nursery to the food bank.

■ Ask them to think about how each one of these might be considered mission, how each one is a way of witnessing for Christ in a world in which most people do not know him well, if at all. Some church programs, such as a food bank, may readily be seen as mission. The challenge will be helping class members see that in an unchurched society, where each congregation is a mission outpost, almost everything we do is mission. Even worship, which in a traditional view would not be seen as mission, takes on that added dimension.

■ Encourage participants to use the space provided on the handout under "_____ Church—A Modern Day Jerusalem" to write their own description of their church as a mission outpost. Perhaps this material could be shared more broadly in the church newsletter or worship bulletin next Sunday.

## Responding

**6.** *Select a mission for further involvement. (5–10 minutes)*

■ Invite the class to review the material you have covered in this session.

■ Suggest that, in order to avoid their being like those who just stood there gazing up into heaven, you would like to challenge them to do something. Perhaps a mission of their own congregation needs to be begun or expanded, or perhaps they would like to discover ways to be more supportive of a national and international mission effort of the denomination.

■ Urge the class to make a decision about one thing they will do to enhance their involvement in mission.

**7.** *Close with a song and prayer. (5 minutes)*

■ Close with a familiar song about being witnesses engaged in mission. "Pass It On," "Here I Am, Lord," and "We've a Story to Tell to the Nations" are possibilities.

■ Close with a prayer asking for God's guidance and power as you seek to become more effective and faithful witnesses.

# APPENDIX A

# Handouts

# Handout #1

# Soul Freedom

**Biblical Basis:** Matthew 16:13–16
**Key Bible Verse:** "Who do you say that I am?"
(Matthew 16:15).

## Soul Freedom

"Our key is this: To understand the Baptists we must see the principle called 'soul freedom.' By this we mean the deep conviction that every man or woman has both the ability and the necessity to enter into direct saving relationship to God through Christ. Baptists believe that this is a personal relationship needing no outside mediation or formation."[1] These are the words Gene Bartlett used to introduce Baptists to those who might not know us very well. If you want to understand us, he seemed to be saying, you need to understand soul freedom. As true as that is, it is also true that many Baptists would be at a loss to describe soul freedom and the way in which it has shaped our life together.

What is this strange-sounding phrase that lies at the very heart of who Baptists are? In brief, soul freedom describes the Baptist belief that each person has both the right and the responsibility to stand before God and to make decisions regarding his or her personal relationship with God. This freedom is a gift of God in creation. A personal relationship with Christ that is not founded on this freedom will always be some-thing less than it should be, something less than God intends for it to be.

Soul freedom is the freedom of every person to discover and respond to the call of God, the freedom to find and follow the will and way of God. Baptists have always recognized that this is something no one can determine for or dictate to another. Soul freedom leads us to resist government involvement in religion, so that each person is free not to pray or to pray in any manner he or she will. Soul freedom leads us to insist on congregational government so that there is no hierarchy imposing its will or its understanding of God's truth upon others.

Working all this out in a context of differing values, divergent understandings of God's will, and different interpretations of God's Word is always difficult. There are no set answers. Even today the attempt to do this creates intense conversations, sometimes even conflict, within churches and Baptist denominations. The principle remains, however. Soul freedom is at the very core of what it means to be a Baptist. It is a heritage we must both celebrate and protect.

From Jeffrey D. Jones, *We Are Baptists: Studies for Adults* (Valley Forge, Pa.: Judson Press, 2001).
Reproduced by permission of the publisher.

## Soul Freedom in the Bible

Look up the following passages. Consider ways in which soul freedom (the right and responsibility to stand before God and make decisions regarding one's relationship with God) is assumed by the story that is told. Use the space provided to make notes on each passage.

**Matthew 16:13–16:**

**Mark 3:31–35:**

**Mark 10:17–22:**

**Mark 14:10–11:**

**Luke 10: 38–42:**

**Genesis 3:1–13:**

**Genesis 12:1–5:**

**Jeremiah 1:4–8:**

# The Basic Baptist Principle

Soul freedom has been called the most basic Baptist principle. That is because many of our historic emphases have their foundation in our belief in soul freedom. Listed below are several historic Baptist emphases. Discuss ways in which you believe soul freedom is basic to each emphasis.

**Believers' baptism**—baptism of those who are old enough to have experienced God's saving grace and make a commitment to relationship with Christ:

**Religious freedom**—no involvement of the state either in establishing or prohibiting religious practice:

**Autonomy of the local church**—the right of each local congregation to order its life and determine its relationships with other churches:

**Priesthood of all believers**—the ability of each believer to stand before God without an intermediary:

## Soul Freedom and Contemporary Issues

In the early decades of the nineteenth century Baptists were divided over the issue of slavery. Some deeply and fervently believed that slavery was a sin, totally incompatible with the will and Word of God. Others believed just as deeply and fervently that slavery was consistent with the teachings of the Bible. Such strongly differing convictions resulted from the application of soul freedom to an important issue of life. For many years, Baptists who strongly disagreed remained together in various mission organizations. By the mid-1840s, however, that was no longer possible. The American Baptist Home Mission Society mandated that no slave holder would be commissioned as a missionary. Churches throughout the South objected to this action and withdrew from the Society to form the Southern Baptist Convention. Was the Society negating the importance of soul freedom as a Baptist principle by rejecting the biblical interpretation of slavery that some Baptists believed in? If so, was it right to do this in response to a higher ethical imperative that they saw as God's will?

### What issues today offer the same challenge to Baptists?

**Note**
1. Gene Bartlett, *These Are the Baptists* (Royal Oak, Mich.: Cathedral Publishers, 1972), 2.

# Handout #2

# Believers' Baptism

**Biblical Basis:** Acts 8:26–40
**Key Bible Verse:** "What is to prevent me from being baptized?" (Acts 8:36).

## The Beginnings of Believers' Baptism

In 1602 John Smyth, a brilliant young Cambridge graduate and city preacher at the Anglican Cathedral of Lincoln in England, renounced from his pulpit the episcopacy of the established church as being unscriptural. Such preaching brought immediate reaction from the authorities, who had Smyth removed from his position. As a result, a small group of Separatists in Gainsborough called him as their pastor. When persecution in England became severe, Smyth and his congregation moved to Holland and in 1606 became the Second English Church at Amsterdam.

John Smyth's devotion to the Word of God drove him to an ever deeper search into Scripture. Two convictions emerged from his study. First, he concluded that the early church was a gathered church composed of those who had knowingly repented of their sins, had found forgiveness, and had accepted Christ as Lord and Savior. Second, he concluded that in the New Testament church only those who had first repented of their sins and confessed their faith in Christ were to be baptized.

In 1609 Smyth and thirty-six members of his congregation affirmed that their infant baptisms were not valid, that they must be baptized as believers, and that the church should be limited to believers. With these declarations, they dissolved their church and Smyth baptized himself and then baptized others upon the profession of their faith. Together they formed the first English-speaking Baptist church.[1]

## Basic Baptist Beliefs about Baptism

*Baptists believe in the baptism of believers.*

*Baptists affirm baptism as a human response to God's action.*

*Baptists practice baptism by immersion.*

From Jeffrey D. Jones, *We Are Baptists: Studies for Adults* (Valley Forge, Pa.: Judson Press, 2001). Reproduced by permission of the publisher.

## Other New Testaments Affirmations about Baptism

Go therefore and make disciples of all nations, baptizing them in the name of the Father and of the Son and of the Holy Spirit, and teaching them to obey everything that I have commanded you. And remember, I am with you always, to the end of the age" (Matthew 28:19–20).

Peter said to them, "Repent, and be baptized every one of you in the name of Jesus Christ so that your sins may be forgiven; and you will receive the gift of the Holy Spirit" (Acts 2:38).

Therefore we have been buried with him by baptism into death, so that, just as Christ was raised from the dead by the glory of the Father, so we too might walk in newness of life (Romans 6:4).

As many of you as were baptized into Christ have clothed yourselves with Christ (Galatians 3:27).

. . .when you were buried with him in baptism, you were also raised with him through faith in the power of God, who raised him from the dead (Colossians 2:12).

For in the one Spirit we were all baptized into one body—Jews or Greeks, slaves or free—and we were all made to drink of one Spirit (1 Corinthians 12:13).

## For Personal Reflection. . .

**What new or renewed affirmations about baptism can you make because of today's discussion?**

**For you right now, are there elements of the meaning of baptism that you would like to make a more meaningful part of your life?**

**Note**
1. Adapted from *The Baptists* by John E. Skoglund (Valley Forge, Pa.: Judson Press, 1967).

# Handout #3

# The Bible

**Biblical Basis:** 2 Timothy 3:14–17
**Key Bible Verse:** "All Scripture is inspired by God and is useful for teaching the truth, rebuking error, correcting faults, and giving instruction for right living" (2 Timothy 3:16, TEV).

## A People of the Book

Baptists are known for their diversity and individualism. They don't believe any pastor or denominational leader can speak for them on matters of faith. They insist that individuals should, with the Holy Spirit's guidance, make up their own minds about what they believe. This does not suggest chaos, as some would contend, or a church with no grounding. Despite their many differences, Baptists are united by a willingness to embrace the Bible as a trustworthy, authoritative, and all-sufficient source for Christian living.

Historian Winthrop Still Hudson captured the essence of Baptists' faithfulness and obedience to God's Word in Christ when he wrote: "The Baptists, as a separate people, date from the early years of the seventeenth century. They were part of the Puritan movement in England, and they had their origin in an essentially 'ecumenical' concern. It was not their basic motivation to be Baptists. They had no desire to identify Baptist 'distinctives.' Their concern and their endeavor was to be faithful and obedient Christians. To this end, they sought to study the mind of Christ as it was disclosed to them in Scripture, to determine what he required of them, and then to order their common life in faithfulness and obedience to him."[1]

### For Discussion

■ Is it a mistake to seek to identify those things that make Baptists different from other Christian groups? Why or why not?

■ On what basis is a church's or an individual's faithfulness to be determined?

■ Baptists, on occasion, have sought to pull out specific passages from Scripture to support particular beliefs and practices. Can this be done with integrity? Explain.

From Jeffrey D. Jones, *We Are Baptists: Studies for Adults* (Valley Forge, Pa.: Judson Press, 2001). Reproduced by permission of the publisher.

## What Do You Believe about the Bible?

On the continuum below, mark the spot that best describes your personal beliefs about the Bible.
You can place yourself anywhere along the continuum.

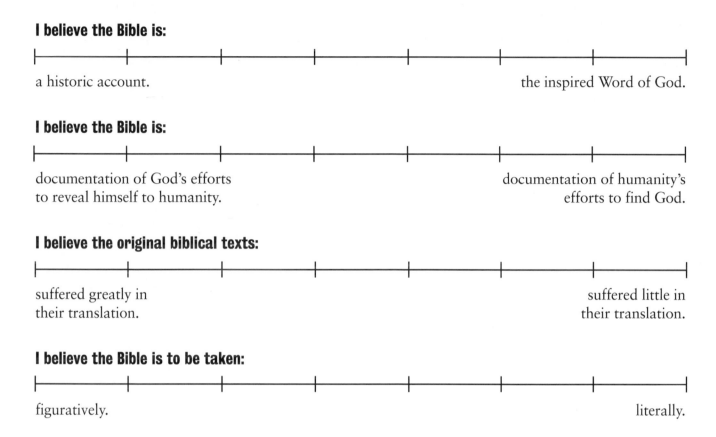

**I believe the Bible is:**

a historic account.

the inspired Word of God.

**I believe the Bible is:**

documentation of God's efforts
to reveal himself to humanity.

documentation of humanity's
efforts to find God.

**I believe the original biblical texts:**

suffered greatly in
their translation.

suffered little in
their translation.

**I believe the Bible is to be taken:**

figuratively.

literally.

## The Bible as God's Word

*The noted biblical scholar Henry H. Halley wrote:*

Apart from any theory of inspiration; or any theory of how the Bible books came to their present form; or how much the text may have suffered in transmission at the hands of editors and copyists; apart from the question of how much is to be interpreted literally and figuratively, or what is historical and what may be poetical; if we all assume that the Bible is just what it appears to be, and study its books to know their contents, we will find there a Unity of Thought indicating that One Mind inspired the writing and compilation of the whole series of books; that it bears on its face the stamp of its Author; that it is in a unique and distinctive sense the word of God.[2]

### For Discussion

■ Do Halley's comments change your thinking about the Bible in any way?

■ Based on what Halley wrote, would you now change your place on the above continuums in any way? Explain.

## Write a Letter

Read silently 2 Timothy 3:14–17. This passage is part of a letter written by the apostle Paul to his friend and colleague, Timothy. At the time the letter was written, Paul was imprisoned in Rome and awaiting execution for a crime he did not commit. The purpose of his letter was to encourage Timothy to remain faithful and be true to God's Word.

What would you say to a friend or family member if you wanted to encourage that person to embrace the Bible as a source of support, inspiration, and guidance for everyday life? Reflect on the Scripture passage for ideas. Then use the space below to write your letter.

## Notes

1. Winthrop Still Hudson, *Baptist Convictions* (Valley Forge, Pa.: Judson Press, 1963), 6.
2. Henry H. Halley, "The Bible Is God's Word," *Halley's Bible Handbook* (Grand Rapids, Mich.: Zondervan Publishing House, 1965), 22.

# Handout #4

# Priesthood of All Believers

**Biblical Basis:** Revelation 1:4–6
**Key Bible Verse:** "[Christ] loves us and freed us from our sins by his blood, and made us to be a kingdom, priests serving his God and Father" (Revelation 1:5–6).

## Every Believer a Minister?

"While we honor the distinct call to vocational ministry, we believe the Bible declares that every believer is a minister."

Noted educator and preacher Russell Dilday, in a 1995 keynote address to a group of Baptists, voiced concern that many of our historic and most cherished Baptist distinctives are in danger of being washed away by those from "inside the family who never knew or have forgotten what our true identity is and are distorting it." He pointed to the "priesthood of all believers" as one of many Baptist hallmarks under fire.

The priesthood of all believers characterizes the understanding among Baptists that the ministry belongs to the whole church. The entire body of believers is called to love and serve God, to bear witness to Jesus Christ, and to care and pray for others. Baptists have no priestly class. Said Dilday: "Our ministers are not essentially different from the laity. . . . Other churches have only a vague line of demarcation between the church and world, but a very sharp line of demarcation between the ministry and the laity. Baptists reverse that. We have a sharp line of demarcation between the church and world, but only a vague line between ministry and laity."

In response to pastors who claim the Scriptures teach that they are the rulers of the church, Dilday said: "That should raise the hackles of every true Baptist. It should stir a righteous rejection of authoritarian styles of pastoral leadership. Lay persons especially should boldly declare, 'We have no hierarchy within our ministry.' While we honor the distinct call to vocational ministry, we believe the Bible declares that every believer is a minister. Let's nail that down. It's the Baptist way."

## For Discussion

■ Do you think the priesthood of all believers is an important concept to uphold within our churches? Why or why not?

■ Explain why you agree or disagree with Dilday's comment that lay persons should reject authoritarian leadership among pastors.

■ If all are equal in the life of the church, does this mean we all have the same gifts? Explain.

From Jeffrey D. Jones, *We Are Baptists: Studies for Adults* (Valley Forge, Pa.: Judson Press, 2001). Reproduced by permission of the publisher.

## Clergy or Laity?

Baptist historians Norman H. Maring and Winthrop S. Hudson point out that all members of the church are ministers, but not all are pastors. The distinction, they say, is one of role and function. There are diverse gifts among God's people and diverse kinds of ministries. "The priesthood of all believers, therefore, does not eliminate the necessity of some division of labor within the church," they write.[1]

Review the following list of ministries. For each one, check whether you think it should be the responsibility of the pastor only, the laity only, or both the pastor and the laity.

| Ministry | Pastor Only | Laity Only | Pastor and Laity |
|---|---|---|---|
| Evangelizing within the community | | | |
| Following up with visitors to the church | | | |
| Presiding at the Communion table | | | |
| Overseeing Christian education programs | | | |
| Preaching from the pulpit on Sundays | | | |
| Leading in prayer during worship | | | |
| Counseling members in times of crisis | | | |
| Baptizing new believers | | | |
| Planning strategies for church growth | | | |
| Overseeing church finances | | | |
| Leading Bible study for the congregation | | | |
| Planning/coordinating mission outreach | | | |
| Reading the Scripture during worship | | | |
| Officiating at wedding ceremonies | | | |
| Officiating at funeral services | | | |

### For Discussion

- Do you think there is a basic difference in the roles and responsibilities of clergy and laity? Explain.

- Could your church function without a pastor? How might your church's ministry be hindered?

- Place a check beside those ministries above that you feel you personally could carry out. What do your responses say about your own sense of call and ministry?

## Responding to God's Call to Ministry

The church does not exist only during those times when people gather for worship or a formal church program. Maring and Hudson write: "The church exists even when its members are dispersed in their homes and at their jobs, and its ministry is carried on through all of the roles and relationships of individual Christians. Not everyone bears his [or her] witness or carries out his [or her] Christian vocation in exactly the same way, but everyone is called to serve Christ in all of his [or her] life"[2]

**Make a list of how you can serve as God's minister in each of the following settings:**

**At home**

**At work**

**At church**

**In the wider community**

**Nationally and globally**

**Notes**

1. Norman H. Maring and Winthrop S. Hudson, *A Baptist Manual of Polity and Practice* (Valley Forge, Pa.: Judson Press, 1963), 94.
2. Ibid., 92–93.

# Handout #5

# Religious Liberty

**Biblical Basis:** Acts 5:17–32
**Key Bible Verse:** "We must obey God rather than any human authority" (Acts 5:29).

## Religious Liberty and the Separation of Church and State

Religious liberty is a theological principle grounded in Scripture. Based in the freedom with which God created us, it is an essential part of human nature and cannot be denied. Separation of church and state is a political doctrine adopted by governments in order to make religious liberty a practical reality. It enables religious freedom to be exercised, but it does not give the freedom. God does. Baptists played an important role in making both the theological principle of religious liberty and the constitutional doctrine of separation of church and state a part of America's fabric of life. From early colonial days Baptists have worked to establish and maintain religious freedom.

Roger Williams was a Baptist for only a few months. Yet he is an important part of our history. He established Rhode Island as a place of religious freedom and helped make Baptists acutely aware of the need for this freedom. Isaac Backus, a Massachusetts Baptist pastor in the eighteenth century, was a tireless proponent of this same freedom before the Continental Congress and in the early days of the nation. John Leland, a Virginia Baptist pastor, played a vitally important role in the effort to secure a Bill of Rights that guaranteed religious freedom.

## Two Perspectives on the Separation of Church and State

One common rationale for separation of church and state was supported by the Enlightenment thinking of Thomas Jefferson and James Madison. Essentially secular in nature, this view supports a "high wall of separation" in order to keep religion at bay. There is, however, another rationale for religious freedom—one that is evangelical in its approach. This view is based in our historic Baptist principle of soul freedom. Soul freedom is the right and responsibility of the individual to stand before God and make decisions regarding his or her relationship with God. In this view the purpose of separation of church and state is not to protect persons *from* religion but to protect them *for* religion. Its purpose is to enable the unfettered development of faith. It seeks to protect both the individual Christian and the church from interference from the state that can thwart vital and vibrant faith.

This has been the historic Baptist view of the need for separation of church and state. It has placed us in the company of those who have a much more secular view of life than we do and has opened us to attacks that we are not truly "religious" or that we do not care about faith. But its foundation rests firmly in the fact that we take faith very seriously, so seriously that we are highly suspicious of any apart from the church who would attempt to define what it is and tell us how to practice it.

From Jeffrey D. Jones, *We Are Baptists: Studies for Adults* (Valley Forge, Pa.: Judson Press, 2001).
Reproduced by permission of the publisher.

# The School Prayer Amendment

The continuing debate over a proposed "school prayer amendment" should be of grave concern to all those who cherish the religious freedom Baptists have supported, suffered for, and even died for over the years.

A proposal to add a "school prayer amendment" to the Constitution has been introduced in the House of Representatives regularly for many years. Sadly, support for this amendment is often based on twisted truth and misunderstood interpretations of both our history and our faith.

The greatest "twisted truth" is that the Supreme Court has "outlawed" prayer in our public schools. Such a statement makes good campaign rhetoric, but like much other campaign rhetoric, it is a lie. The Court has done no such thing. A humorous response to this claim is to point out that as long as there are math tests there will always be prayer in public schools. But this humor also reveals a great truth: it is impossible to outlaw prayer—in school or any place else.

Another erroneous claim is that somehow our rights as Christians are being taken away by the Court. But in fact the only restriction placed on Christians in the school activities is that they cannot be disruptive. Groups of students can meet and pray at school. Public schools must grant student religious groups the same meeting privileges as other extracurricular groups.

What the Supreme Court has said is that mandated prayer, or prayer provided for by school authorities, violates the First Amendment's provision of religious freedom. Certainly it does that if children are coerced into praying to a God they don't believe in. That coercion can come from peer pressure and the fear of being different, as well as through a mandated time of prayer.

But an even deeper concern to me is the impact mandated school prayer would have on our faith.

As a person of deep faith convictions I do not want to let school authorities develop a "non-sectarian" prayer for my children to pray. That is not their business and to give them that authority is to threaten the freedom all of us have to pray to God in our own ways and words.

At bottom, all of this makes a mockery of prayer. It would reduce it to a recited ritual of lowest common denominator claptrap. Generic prayer is no prayer at all. For our children to be asked by government authorities to pray such a prayer would be an insult to our faith and to God.

There is no doubt that prayer is needed both in and for this nation and its people. But the responsibility for that rests in our churches and other religious institutions and in the people who claim a faith that believes in prayer. To turn that concern into advocacy for a constitutional amendment to "protect" prayer is to fight the wrong battle in the wrong place over the wrong issue.

## For Discussion

■ What is your initial reaction to this article?

■ If it had appeared in your church's newsletter, what would you have done?

■ In what ways do you agree with the writer? In what ways do you disagree?

■ Where do you see evidence of both the secular and evangelical perspectives on separation of church and state in the article?

■ Which perspective do you think is most important for Christians today?

■ If you were to write an article about the proposed school prayer amendment what would you say? Why?

## Resources and Action Possibilities

Listed below are several resources that will help you learn more about and become more involved in the concern for religious freedom. Select one resource you would like to get in order to explore this topic more fully. After you receive and read it, share what you have learned with class members.

The Baptist Joint Committee on Public Affairs is a cooperative body that acts as a Baptist voice on issues of church and state. It offers a variety of resources that can be helpful in understanding both the historical and contemporary concerns related to religious liberty. These include:

■ "Report from the Capital," a newsletter providing updates on contemporary church-state issues. Subscription cost is $10 per year.

■ "Life with Liberty Series," a pamphlet series that highlights a Baptist perspective on concerns such as religious freedom, Christianity in Ameri-can life, government intrusion into religion, and religion in public schools. Up to nine copies are available free.

■ "Religion in the Public Schools: A Joint Statement of Current Law." Developed by a wide range of groups, including the National Association of Evangelicals, the National Council of Churches, the American Jewish Committee, and the American Muslim Council, this brochure is an excellent statement of what is and isn't permitted in public schools, as well as student religious rights that schools must protect.

The address for the Baptist Joint Committee is 200 Maryland Ave., NE, Washington, DC 20002; phone 202-544-4226; e-mail bjcpa@erols.com. Further information about the committee's resources and activities is available on its website: www.erols.com\bjcpa.

# Handout #6

# Autonomy of the Local Church

**Biblical Basis:** Acts 2:40–47
**Key Bible Verse:** "They devoted themselves to the apostles' teaching and fellowship, to the breaking of bread and prayers" (Acts 2:42).

## What Is Congregational Autonomy?

Baptists have a different understanding of the church than most people. For Baptists, the local congregation is the key. This local congregation is representative of the whole church of Jesus Christ. It is free to govern its own affairs, to order its worship, to decide how and with which other churches it will relate. And yet, Baptist churches are not just isolated congregations. From the earliest times they have seen the need to gather in associations to do things they cannot do alone and to seek counsel and advice from one another. There have been times these two realities, autonomy and cooperation, have created tension among Baptists as they have sought to balance them appropriately in the midst of sometimes contentious issues. The principles remain valid, however. It is those principles that are the focus of this session.

Congregational autonomy is "the right of each congregation (1) to choose its own ministers and officers, (2) to establish its own covenant membership and discipline and confessions, (3) to order its life in its own organizational forms with its constitution and bylaws, (4) to implement its right to belong to other denominational agencies and ecumenical church bodies, (5) to own and to control its own property and budget."[1]

"Church freedom is the historic Baptist affirmation that local churches are free, under the Lordship of Jesus Christ, to determine their membership and leadership, to order their worship and work, to ordain whom they perceive as gifted for ministry, male or female, and to participate in the larger Body of Christ, of whose unity and mission Baptists are proudly a part."[2]

From Jeffrey D. Jones, *We Are Baptists: Studies for Adults* (Valley Forge, Pa.: Judson Press, 2001).
Reproduced by permission of the publisher.

# Three Ways of Organizing the Church

*Which diagram below best illustrates each of the following organizational styles?*

## Congregational
The basis of the congregational system is the local congregation, which makes all decisions regarding its own life, organization, and practice. Decisions are made by members of the congregation within boundaries and according to procedures it has established.

What advantages and disadvantages do you see to this way of organizing?

## Presbyterian
In a presbyterian system, authority rests in a grouping of churches, usually known as a presbytery. Local congregations relate to it, and many decisions of the congregation, such as the calling of the pastor, must be confirmed by the presbytery. A book of order governs much of congregational life and practice.

What advantages and disadvantages do you see to this way of organizing?

## Episcopal
An episcopal system rests on the authority of bishops, who provide guidance and direction for the life and ministry of local congregations. The bishop and councils of bishops hold the authority to appoint clergy, to adopt creeds, and to determine ways in which the work of congregations will be ordered.

What advantages and disadvantages do you see to this way of organizing?

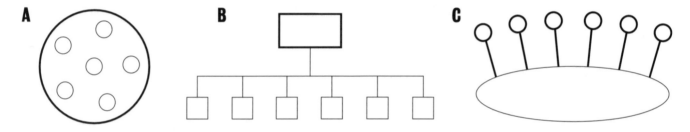

# The Responsibility That Goes with Freedom

With the freedom of congregational autonomy comes great responsibility. It is the responsibility of being the church—of listening for and responding to God's call so that the congregation will remain faithful in its life and ministry. No one can tell a local Baptist congregation what it must be and do except God. It is the congregation's responsibility to listen and obey when God speaks. This means each local congregation needs to develop a listening stance, refusing to be so caught up in its own issues and survival that it cannot hear the voice of God. The congregation must constantly be open to change, willing to move in new directions when God calls, and it must be willing to risk, seeing and doing things differently from others because of its sense of God's will. Each local congregation has this responsibility. It cannot rely on bishops or outside structures to tell it what to do in order to be faithful. It must claim the responsibility of faithfulness for itself.

■ In what ways do you see your own congregation exercising that responsibility?

■ How is this different than it would be for a church that had a presbyterian or episcopal form of government?

■ What are the things that get in the way of our hearing and responding to God's call?

■ What might your congregation do to be even more responsible in its attention to God's will for it?

74

## The Way We Relate

### Baptist

_____ Association _____

_____ Region _____

_____ National _____

_____ International _____

_____ Other _____

### Ecumenical

_____ Local _____

_____ Regional _____

_____ National _____

_____ International _____

_____ Other _____

### Notes

1. William H. Keucher, "Congregational Autonomy," _Baptist Leader,_ March 1976, p. 49.
2. Walter B. Shurden, _The Baptist Identity: Four Fragile Freedoms_ (Macon, Ga.: Smyth and Helwys Publishing, Inc., 1993), 33.

# Handout #7

# Ministry of the Laity

**Biblical Basis:** Ephesians 4:1–7,11–13
**Key Bible Verse:** ". . . for the work of ministry, for building up the body of Christ . . ."
(Ephesians 4:12).

## The Letter to the Ephesians

The concern of the Letter to the Ephesians is nothing less than the redemption of all creation. You can't get much bigger in scope than that! In the letter's view, redemption is God's plan. It is what the work of Christ was and is all about. As the body of Christ, the church continues that work. This is where the ministry of the laity comes in. The ministry of the *laos,* the people of God, is to join in the work of redemption, not just of themselves, but of all creation.

This is easier said than done. After a bold affirmation in the first chapter, much of the rest of the letter explains how redemption happens through the church and in the lives of Christians. The passage that is our focus in this session comes from the section of the letter that deals with the church.

At the time the letter was written, there was no clear notion of ordination in the church. The specific roles mentioned in this passage were for *everyone,* not just clergy. Any disciple might be an apostle, prophet, evangelist, pastor, or teacher. The key was simply whether or not the person had the specific gifts needed to fulfill one of these roles. The primary focus of prophets, pastors, and teachers was most often inside the church. That of the apostles and evangelists, however, was often outside. Similarly, ministry could be both within the church and to the community and world.

The Bible passage does not offer a clear description or definition of ministry of the laity; the idea had no place in a time when there was no formalized process of ordination, no separation of clergy and laity. The passage does provide, however, a solid underpinning for this historic Baptist principle. It affirms three basic concepts that continue to be important for us today: (1) Christ gave a variety of gifts; (2) these gifts are to be used to enable others in ministry; and (3) this ministry belongs to all the people of God, both clergy and laity, and takes place both inside and outside the church.

From Jeffrey D. Jones, *We Are Baptists: Studies for Adults* (Valley Forge, Pa.: Judson Press, 2001). Reproduced by permission of the publisher.

# Helen Barrett Montgomery

Helen Barrett Montgomery was born in 1861 in the small town of Kingston, Ohio. Both of her parents were teachers. When Helen was seven, her father became the principal of an academy in Lowville, New York. Then, in 1871, the family moved again, this time to Rochester, New York, where her father became principal of the Collegiate Institute. Shortly after the move, her father resigned as principal in order to attend Rochester Divinity School. Upon graduation in 1876 he became pastor of Lake Avenue Baptist Church in Rochester. This church was to remain the central influence in Helen's life.

When she was fifteen, Helen was baptized by her father and quickly became very involved in the life of the church. She taught a boys' Sunday school class at church and a class for at-risk boys at a nearby mission, and she was active in the young people's group. In the fall of 1880, Helen began her freshman year at the recently founded Wellesley College. After graduation, she followed in her father's footsteps to become a teacher.

In 1887 she returned to Rochester and married William A. Montgomery. Together they shared a life of love, faith, and service for more than forty years. Her sense of special calling by God was expressed in a letter written to her parents at the time of her marriage: "I am growing more and more anxious that my life may be given without reserve to God's service. As Will said, if we start out with the purpose of always doing the very highest thing we know, we must have a great deal of courage and honest conviction, for it would often be a hard thing to achieve. Before he went away he knelt down with me and together we consecrated our lives to God's work in the world, promising to make this work our first thought and asking His strength to keep us unspotted from the world."[1]

This commitment led Helen into a remarkable life of service to Christ, the church, and others. She was instrumental in opening the University of Rochester to female students. She was the first woman elected to the Rochester Board of Education. She was a prolific writer, especially in the area of world mission, and traveled extensively to see firsthand the work of missionaries. This interest led to her election as president of the Woman's American Baptist Foreign Mission Society and then as president of the Northern Baptist Convention. Upon her election in 1921 she became the first woman to hold this office, serving with skill and grace during a time of significant denominational conflict. Helen's love of Greek and her desire to reach people with Christ led her to translate the New Testament into contemporary English.

In her personal and public life, in her life within and outside the church, Helen remains a profound example of one who takes the call of God seriously and lets it shape all of life.

## For Discussion

■ What specific ministries did Helen Barrett Montgomery pursue?

■ Which of these took place inside the church, which outside?

■ How are all of these activities "ministry"?

■ Do you think Helen Barrett Montgomery was "called" to these ministries in the same way clergy are called? If not, how was her calling different?

## Ministry of the Laity

*Ministry of the laity affirms the importance of participation of the laity in what are often seen as "clergy" responsibilities.* Members of the laity share in pastoral care, as well as in leadership in worship. They preside at the Lord's table, offering prayers of thanks and blessing for the bread and cup. They respond to God's call to minister to others—children, youth, and adults, who are a part of the community of faith—in ways similar to the care extended to widows and orphans by the early church. They nurture each other in the faith and their relationship with Christ, becoming priests to one another.

*Ministry of the laity also affirms the ministry each disciple has in the world.* In these various ministries members of the laity use their God-given gifts as they respond to God's call to serve others in the name of Christ. The particular nature of the ministry varies greatly. It may be within the family, as mother or father. It may be job-related, to serve others in business or a profession. It may be a call to volunteer service, providing needed support to the community and its members. It may be a call that has political implications or that leads to social action. Whatever its exact form, ministry begins with a stirring in the heart, as sense of calling from God, that directs us into a particular role, not just because we want to be there, but because we believe that this is what God intends for us to do.

*The implications of this understanding of ministry of the laity for the congregation are significant.* The concept of ministry of the laity emphasizes the importance of the congregational role in helping members discover, develop, and use their gifts. It implies that becoming sensitive to the call of God in their lives is a primary concern for all Christians. It suggests that churches whose internal structure demands so much time and effort that there is little left for other things undercut their members' ability to respond to God's call to ministry of the laity in the world!

### Note

1. From a pamphlet by Conda Delite Hitch Abbott, "Envoy of Grace: The Life of Helen Barrett Montgomery," published by the American Baptist Historical Society (Valley Forge, Pa.), n.d.

# Handout #8

# Discipleship

**Biblical Basis:** Colossians 1:27–29
**Key Bible Verse:** ". . . to bring each one into
God's presence as a mature individual in union
with Christ" (Colossians 1:28, TEV).

**A disciple is a person who seeks to learn more about and follow
more fully the teaching and way of life of another.**

## Three Elements of Discipleship

**Deepening spiritual life** speaks of the need for disciples to continue to grow in their personal relationship with Christ. Any relationship, including one with Christ, requires work. In fact, in some ways a relationship with Christ may be more difficult because there is no flesh-and-blood person we can sit down and talk with. What this relationship has going for it, however, is Christ's constant seeking us out, his constant love, and his constant desire to have a relationship with us.

- What are the methods you use to grow in your relationship with Christ?

- What other ways are provided by your church?

- What are some of the signs of "Christ in us" that we can note in ourselves and others?

From Jeffrey D. Jones, *We Are Baptists: Studies for Adults* (Valley Forge, Pa.: Judson Press, 2001).
Reproduced by permission of the publisher.

**Equipping** speaks of the need to continue to develop the attributes that make faithful living possible. For Christians, a key to equipping is found in the discovery and development of our God-given gifts. Being equipped then is the ongoing process of discovering and developing gifts. Equipping also includes acquiring knowledge and skills. In order to be disciples of Jesus Christ, we need to know who he is and what he tells us about how we are to live. That knowledge comes primarily through Bible study. Living as faithful disciples may also require the use of particular skills, such as preaching, leadership, working with youth, carpentry, or cooking. The list is limitless. It all depends on the ways in which we have been called to live out our discipleship.

■ How have you discovered and begun to use your God-given gifts?

■ In what ways does your church provide Bible study that enables people to know who Christ is and what he tells us about how we are to live?

**Ministering** speaks of the need to put faith into action by responding to God's call to serve others in the name of Jesus Christ. Ministering is a fulfillment of our call, but it also enables continuing growth as disciples. Deepening spiritual life, equipping, and involvement in ministry are interconnected. The further we follow Christ in ministering, the deeper our relationship with him grows and the more we are equipped to serve in his name. The more all three of these happen, the more faithful disciples we become.

■ In what ways might skills that you have be used specifically as a way of living out your discipleship?

■ In what ways does engaging in active ministry also deepen our relationship with Christ?

# Discipleship Growth Chart

|  | **What's Involved** | **What I'm Doing** | **What I Could Do** |
|---|---|---|---|
| **Deepening** | | | |
| **Equipping** | | | |
| **Ministering** | | | |

**Help me, God, to grow as a disciple by** _____

_____ .

# Handout #9

# Evangelism

**Biblical Basis:** Acts 3:1–16
**Key Bible Verse:** "I have no silver or gold, but what I have I give you; in the name of Jesus Christ of Nazareth, stand up and walk" (Acts 3:6).

## Evangelism is . . .

|  | Me | Church |
|---|---|---|
| the joyous witness of the People of God to the redeeming love of God | | |
| urging all to repent | | |
| and to be reconciled to God and each other | | |
| through faith in Jesus Christ who lived, died, and was raised from the dead, | | |
| so that | | |
| being made new and empowered by the Holy Spirit | | |
| believers are incorporated as disciples into the church for worship, fellowship, nurture and engagement in God's mission of evangelism and liberation within society and creation, | | |
| signifying the Kingdom which is present and yet to come.[1] | | |

From Jeffrey D. Jones, *We Are Baptists: Studies for Adults* (Valley Forge, Pa.: Judson Press, 2001).
Reproduced by permission of the publisher.

## Biblical Insights on Evangelists

| | Me | Church |
|---|---|---|

Evangelists understand that the gospel comes to people as a response to human need.

Evangelists understand both what they can offer to others and what they cannot.

Evangelists are willing to risk in order make the Good News real.

Evangelists are clear about the power behind the Good News.

Evangelists understand that all people have complete freedom to respond or not respond to the Good News.

## Two Baptist Evangelists

### John Mason Peck, 1789–1858

The time was the early 1800s. The place was any place west of the Allegheny Mountains, a mission field that produced the great need for evangelism. A response to that need began in the heart of John Mason Peck, a New York farmer and pastor.

Eager to be about this work, he headed off to St. Louis with his wife, Sallie, and their three children in 1817—spending 128 days in a wagon and assorted boats. When they arrived, Peck was so ill he had to be carried ashore. Once out of his sickbed, however, he made up for lost time. In the rough and wild town, he rented a room in the back of a store in which to hold worship services and run a school. A year later, crowds gathered along the Mississippi, more out of curiosity than commitment, to watch as Peck baptized his first two converts. During these days he developed patterns of work that would continue for decades to come: a farm at home, a church to pastor, a school to teach in. And the travel—thousands upon thousands of cold, wet, hungry, and often painful miles over the years—to share the Good News, to distribute Bibles and religious tracts, and to establish some kind of continuing organization in each town. It might be a church, a Sunday school, a mission society, a school, or a Bible study club—whatever would work in that particular town, just so there would be an organized group to keep the cause of Christ alive.

When the American Baptist Home Mission Society was founded in 1832, Peck was commissioned as its first missionary. By the time of his death in 1858 he could look back on a land transformed by his efforts. More than any other single man, he is the one who brought religion and learning to the early 1800s frontier. He was a consistent and vocal supporter of abolition and temperance. He was instrumental in the founding of countless churches, Sunday schools, mission societies, and Bible study groups and in developing a system of itinerant preachers in Illinois, public schools throughout Illinois and Missouri, a Baptist newspaper, a college, and a national missionary society.

**83**

## Lulu Fleming, 1862–1899

Lulu Fleming's grandfather had been brought to America from the Congo. She was born into a slave family in Florence, Florida. Her father, though he was a slave, left his family to fight in the Union Army during the Civil War and never returned home. Lulu, with the ongoing help and support of her mother, received an education. At fourteen, she was converted and began teaching in Sunday school. A visiting pastor from the North was so impressed with her ability that he arranged for her to attend Shaw University. She was class valedictorian at graduation. She then returned to Florida to teach public school.

For Lulu Fleming, accepting Christ was about much more than being a believer. Along with the acceptance of Christ came acknowledgment of a responsibility to teach others about him so they might be free through his salvation. When the Women's American Baptist Foreign Mission Society asked for women to serve as missionaries, Lulu knew this call was for her and she responded. In 1886 she became the Society's first woman of African descent commissioned for missionary service.

After her commissioning Lulu set sail for her assigned mission field in the Congo. There she taught school, but her strongest desire was to be free to work in the town and jungle, evangelizing men and women. She developed the practice of teaching all morning and spending the afternoon visiting with the women of the village in their huts. Illness forced her to return to the United States in 1891 after four years in the Congo. With her on the trip were several Congolese students, whom she helped to attend her alma

mater. Having recognized the great medical needs in Africa, Lulu decide to spend her time in the United States studying medicine.

In 1895, Lulu returned to the Congo as a medical missionary; however, she was soon stricken with "sleeping sickness" and had to return to the United States once again. She remained hopeful that she would be able to go back to Africa, but her illness progressed further and she died in 1899.

The number of years Lulu Fleming served as a missionary were not many. But the people she touched and healed and to whom she brought the Good News of Christ were very many. Perhaps even more, her legacy continues to inspire and challenge today. The odds she overcame, the trails she forged, the love she showed make her a model of what an evangelist can be.

## Note
1. American Baptist Policy Statement on Evangelism, adopted June 1984.

# Handout #10

# Worship

**Biblical Basis:** Psalm 95:1–7a
**Key Bible Verse:** "O come, let us worship and bow down,
let us kneel before the LORD, our Maker!" (Psalm 95:6).

## Worship—What Do You Prefer?

Believe it or not, when it comes to worship many of our preferences are influenced by the year in which we were born. One survey of church members showed that those born prior to World War II generally consider worship as meditation, while those born after that war generally consider it celebration. This can make a big difference in what we think is appropriate for a worship service.

*If we believe worship is primarily meditation . . .*
  a quiet time for personal preparation before worship is essential.
  children can be a disruption.
  a sermon that prompts personal contemplation is just right.
  prayers of confession play a central role.

*But if we think worship is primarily celebration . . .*
  a joyous time of community sharing makes sense.
  children can help set the proper tone.
  that same sermon can destroy the essential mood.
  prayers of thanksgiving are most important.

## Insights of Psalm 95

1   O come, let us sing to the LORD;
      let us make a joyful noise to the rock of our salvation!
2   Let us come into his presence with thanksgiving;
      let us make a joyful noise to him with songs of praise!
3   For the LORD is a great God,
      and a great King above all gods.
4   In his hand are the depths of the earth;
      the heights of the mountains are his also.
5   The sea is his, for he made it,
      and the dry land, which his hands have formed.
6   O come, let us worship and bow down,
      let us kneel before the LORD, our Maker!
7   For he is our God,
      and we are the people of his pasture
      and the sheep of his hand.

From Jeffrey D. Jones, *We Are Baptists: Studies for Adults* (Valley Forge, Pa.: Judson Press, 2001).
Reproduced by permission of the publisher.

■ **Verses 1 and 2** extend the invitation to worship God. Verses 3–5 tell us why this is the right thing to do. What are the reasons offered?

■ **Verses 6 and 7a** repeat this pattern. What additional reason is offered?

■ **Verses 1 and 2** suggest several possible elements of worship. What are they?

■ **Verses 3–5 and 7** make several affirmations about what God has done and who God is. What are they?

■ **Verse 3** affirms that God is "a great King above all gods." If God is the only god there is, why is this statement made? What difference does this make to our worship of God?

## The Central Focus of Worship

"There will be no renewal in mainline Protestantism until its worship of God is redeemed from such silliness and the secularization it reflects. . . . The antidote to this secularization is restoring the integrity of the center of worship—the praise of God. . . . There are indeed positive, constructive, liberating, healing, and enlightening consequences of the worship of God. We do get perspective on ourselves and the world, and we do become motivated to address its wrongs. But the utilitarian mind gets the priorities wrong by making the by-product the main product. It forgets, and perhaps denies, that the worship of God is an end in itself."[1]

## The Four Gifts of Worship

These four gifts of worship are suggested by Kennon Callahan in his book *Dynamic Worship*. When have you received these gifts through worship in your life? Talk about these experiences with others in your group, sharing how the gifts were received.

**Power**—Through praise we develop the sense of who and whose we are that gives power to our living.

**Community**—It is the community that worships, but worship also builds community through the common experience of praise.

**Meaning**—Through worship we discover and affirm what is truly important.

**Hope**—Through the celebration of Christ's resurrection we see beyond the hurt and struggle of life.

## What Makes Worship Baptist?

Listed below are a number of commonly agreed-upon Baptist emphases. Check the ones you believe provide a common thread for worship in Baptist churches.

_____ The autonomy of the local congregation

_____ The centrality of the Bible in our life and faith

_____ The priesthood of all believers

_____ Religious liberty

_____ Separation of church and state

_____ Acceptance of baptism and Communion as the only two ordinances

_____ A commitment to mission and evangelism

_____ The presence and the power of the Holy Spirit

## A Note from Baptist History

Baptists have a long history of being concerned about worship. In the seventeenth century, Obadiah Holmes journeyed from his home in Rhode Island to visit a friend who lived in Massachusetts. While there he helped lead a worship service in his friend's home. For that he was arrested, tried, convicted and received twenty lashes. While Baptists today don't have to prove it by subjecting themselves to a whipping, let us hope that the worship of God still holds the importance for them that it did for Obadiah Holmes!

**Note**
1. Leander Keck, *The Church Confident* (Nashville: Abingdon, 1993), 26–27.

# Handout #11

# Issues of Faith

**Biblical Basis:** Acts 4:23–31
**Key Bible Verse:** "When they had prayed . . . they were all filled with the Holy Spirit and spoke the word of God with boldness" (Acts 4:31).

## A People Who Speak Out

It takes boldness to speak God's word, because even though it is a word of salvation based in God's great love for us, it does not always sit well with those who hear it.

From our earliest days, Baptists have taken stands on issues of faith. Early Baptists learned that taking a stand on issues can be a difficult thing to do. Obadiah Holmes was whipped in Massachusetts for speaking God's word in a worship service held in a friend's home. Other Baptists were ridiculed and jailed for speaking in opposition to state-supported churches. Despite the difficulties, the Baptist tradition of taking a stand continues today in local churches, in regional gatherings, and in national denominational meetings.

This is not an easy thing to do. Sometimes God's word for a particular situation or issue is not clear. Sometimes people of deep faith disagree over what that word might be. Sometimes we do not say anything because we are not clear what word needs to be spoken.

Despite the difficulty and disagreements, Christians are called to speak boldly. Baptist history contains many examples of people who boldly spoke God's word. Isaac Backus spoke boldly for the separation of church and state. Prudence Crandall boldly established a school for African American women in Connecticut before the Civil War. Helen Barrett Montgomery was the first woman member of the Rochester, New York, school board, the first woman president of American Baptists, and a translator of the New Testament in a time when women did not do such things. Edwin Dahlberg boldly spoke against the evil of war. Jennie Clare Adams boldly served in a Philippine hospital and was killed with several other missionaries during World War II. Martin Luther King Jr. spoke eloquently and boldly of a dream he had for all God's people. Individual boldness is not easy. It is a great responsibility. Sometimes it is hard to discern the difference between our opinion and God's word. Sometimes we falsely assume that God has no word to speak because we can't "hear" one. Sometimes, like Jonah, we run and hide.

Our tradition as Baptists inspires and challenges us to speak God's word boldly—even when it is difficult, even when the response may not be positive. As people of faith we have a responsibility to interpret and proclaim, to witness, and to defend the mighty works God is doing in our world.

From Jeffrey D. Jones, *We Are Baptists: Studies for Adults* (Valley Forge, Pa.: Judson Press, 2001). Reproduced by permission of the publisher.

# Issues for the Church

For each of the items, make a mark on the continuum to indicate how strongly you agree or disagree.

## The church (locally, regionally, and nationally) should speak out on issues related to:

### Personal morality

Strongly agree                                                                                          Strongly disagree

### Economic conditions

Strongly agree                                                                                          Strongly disagree

### Political candidates

Strongly agree                                                                                          Strongly disagree

### Welfare

Strongly agree                                                                                          Strongly disagree

### Business practices

Strongly agree                                                                                          Strongly disagree

### Capital punishment

Strongly agree                                                                                          Strongly disagree

### Government budget priorities

Strongly agree                                                                                          Strongly disagree

### Evangelism

Strongly agree                                                                                          Strongly disagree

### Medical care and insurance coverage

Strongly agree                                                                                          Strongly disagree

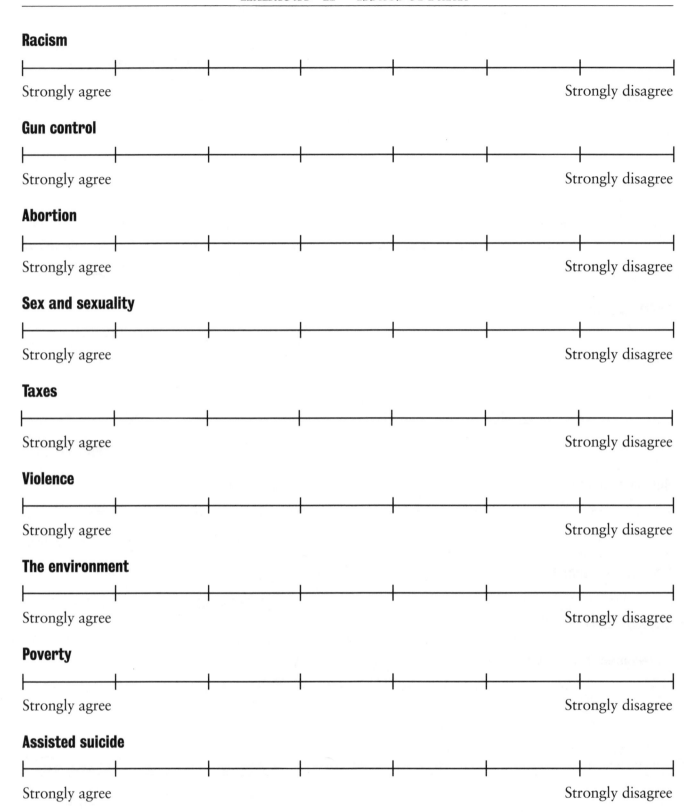

**Racism**

Strongly agree                                                                 Strongly disagree

**Gun control**

Strongly agree                                                                 Strongly disagree

**Abortion**

Strongly agree                                                                 Strongly disagree

**Sex and sexuality**

Strongly agree                                                                 Strongly disagree

**Taxes**

Strongly agree                                                                 Strongly disagree

**Violence**

Strongly agree                                                                 Strongly disagree

**The environment**

Strongly agree                                                                 Strongly disagree

**Poverty**

Strongly agree                                                                 Strongly disagree

**Assisted suicide**

Strongly agree                                                                 Strongly disagree

# Prophetic Role

**Biblical Basis:** 1 Peter 2:1–12
**Key Bible Verse:** "You are a chosen race, a royal priesthood, a holy nation, God's own people, in order that you may proclaim the mighty acts of him who called you out of darkness into his marvelous light" (1 Peter 2:9).

**A prophet is a person who speaks or acts out God's word for a particular people, time, and place.**
The gift of the prophet is to discern the way God is at work in the world and to share that with others. This can be related both to a personal issue in someone's life and to important social and/or political issues in society.

Who were, who are, the prophets who are important to you?

## Three Baptist Prophets

### Walter Rauschenbusch

Walter Rauschenbusch was one of the most important theologians of the social gospel. He was more than just a thinker and a writer; he was a doer. His active ministry shaped his thinking, and his thinking then helped shape his ministry.

Born in 1861, the son of a minister, sixth in a line of ministers, Rauschenbusch became a committed Christian about the age of sixteen. Soon after, he decided to study to become a minister. Originally he had hoped to be a foreign missionary, but he was turned down for work in India. He then interviewed for the position of pastor in a large urban church in the Midwest, but he was not called to that position, either.

A small, struggling church in New York City wanted him as their pastor, however. In 1889 he was called to the Second German Baptist Church in the Hell's Kitchen section of the city. Crime, poverty, and disease were the realities of everyday life there. He served the church for eleven years. The experiences of the people touched his heart deeply. "When I saw how men toiled all their lifelong, hard, toilsome lives, and at the end had almost nothing to show for it, how strong men begged for work and could not get it; how little children died—oh! The children's funerals! They gripped my heart."[1]

*(continued on page 90)*

From Jeffrey D. Jones, *We Are Baptists: Studies for Adults* (Valley Forge, Pa.: Judson Press, 2001).
Reproduced by permission of the publisher.

*(continued from page 89)*

During this time, he began to envision a program for social action based in the gospel. In the Bible he found a deep compassion for the oppressed by a God who stood for justice and righteousness. With this came a calling to minister not just to the individual but to society as a whole.

In 1897 he joined the faculty of Rochester Seminary, which is now Colgate Rochester Divinity School. There he further developed his ideas. He shared them with students through his teaching and with others through his writing. His work was strongly opposed by those who did not believe that the social conditions of the world should be the concern of the church. Rauschenbusch died in July 1918, just as World War I was drawing to a close.

## Isabel Crawford

Isabel Crawford was born in Ontario, Canada, in 1865, the daughter of a Baptist minister who served churches in both Canada and the United States. A severe childhood illness left her with very little hearing. At age eleven she had a conversion experience that led to a deep concern for others, especially the poor of the cities. She graduated from Baptist Missionary Training School, expecting to receive an appointment to city mission work. The appointment that came, however, was to work among Native Americans in Oklahoma. By her own account, she cried for several days after hearing the news. But then, deciding that the appointment was God's will, she devoted herself to the work.

Her first position was on a reservation eighty-seven miles from the nearest railroad. Within a few years she moved to an even more isolated place called Saddle Mountain and began her most significant work. There she shared the gospel, her possessions, and herself in an effort to bring the love of Christ to those she came to love herself. She began a church and led in the construction of a church building. Believing that all Christians were called to give to others, she began a missionary society that would support other mission work. When government supplies failed to arrive on time, she became an articulate and forceful advocate for the Native American cause.

Her ministry among the Kiowas ended in controversy. The church was located far from any ordained clergy. On one Communion Sunday, at her suggestion, the church voted unanimously to let Lucius Aitson, her earliest convert, preside at the Communion service. Affronted by this deci-

sion, the pastors of the local association adopted a resolution of censure. The church was reported to the Home Mission Society and threatened with expulsion from the association. In order to avoid further conflict, Crawford resigned her position and ended her ministry with the Kiowas. The remainder of her life was spent in mission and deputation work. When she died in 1961, her body was returned to Saddle Mountain. Her grave is marked with the simple inscription, "I dwell among my own people." The one the Kiowas called a "Jesus Woman" and named *Geehhoangomah* ("she gave us the Jesus way") had come home.

## Jitsuo Morikawa

Jitsuo Morikawa was born in British Columbia on May 1, 1912. He moved to the United States for his education and received a bachelor of arts degree from Southern Baptist Seminary in Louisville, Kentucky. During World War II he spent eighteen months in the Poston Relocation Center with other Japanese Americans who were placed there simply because of their race. Later, he said that the faithfulness of his own denomination and the American Friends Service Committee in championing the cause of Japanese Americans made an undeniable impact upon his life and future ministry.

Following his forced relocation to Poston, Morikawa spent twelve years as pastor of the First Baptist Church of Chicago. There he directed the church's involvement in the first major urban renewal program on the American scene. He later served as director of evangelism for the American Baptist Convention. He was one of the denomination's best-known and best-loved leaders. He was also a controversial figure, largely because of his quiet and intellectual nature and his belief that the gospel had direct meaning for social and political issues. Morikawa believed that institutions, like individuals, sin and therefore need to be converted to Christ.

After his retirement from denominational leadership, Morikawa served as interim pastor of Riverside Church in New York City and then as pastor of First Baptist Church in Ann Arbor, Michigan. This church was near the campus of the University of Michigan, where he was instrumental in opening a new dialogue between churches and the academic community. He died in July 1987.

# Exploring God's Prophetic Word

■ Which image of God's people speaks most powerfully to you? Why?

_____ living stones (v. 5) _____

_____ a chosen race (v. 9) _____

_____ a royal priesthood (v. 9) _____

_____ a holy nation (v. 9) _____

_____ aliens and exiles (v. 11) _____

■ In what ways do you think Christians are "aliens and exiles" (v. 11) in today's world?

■ Which of the following do you believe should be included among God's "mighty acts" (v. 9)?

| Yes | No | | Why? |
|---|---|---|---|
| _____ | _____ | sending Jesus Christ into the world | _____ |
| _____ | _____ | the founding of the church | _____ |
| _____ | _____ | the establishment of your local congregation | _____ |
| _____ | _____ | the community outreach of your church | _____ |
| _____ | _____ | the effort to outlaw land mines | _____ |
| _____ | _____ | the abolitionist movement before the Civil War | _____ |
| _____ | _____ | gun control efforts | _____ |
| _____ | _____ | welfare reform | _____ |
| _____ | _____ | cutting income taxes | _____ |
| | | others: | _____ |

# Note

1. Quoted by Frank T. Hoadley and Benjamin P. Browne in *Baptists Who Dared* (Valley Forge, Pa.: Judson Press, 1980), 81.

# Handout #13

# Diversity

**Biblical Basis:** Acts 10:34–35; Galatians 3:26–29

**Key Bible Verse:** "So there is no difference between Jews and Gentiles, between slaves and free men, between men and women; you are all one in union with Christ Jesus" (Galatians 3:28, TEV).

Diversity is and always has been a reality. People are different—in dress, values, skin color, and language. Even Christians have differences. We have a variety of ideas about what meaningful worship is and about the church and its purpose. Every day we are confronted by the differences that abound in the world and are thus challenged to search for common bonds that bring us together. When we find common bonds, it becomes easier for us to affirm our differences rather than fear them. This is true in society. It is also true in churches. We are becoming more diverse. For example, while once predominately white, American Baptist Churches, USA, may soon be a denomination in which no racial/ethnic group has majority status. Statistics can't tell the whole story, but they do help us begin to see the picture of a new and growing reality. In 1995 resident membership of American Baptist churches was 53 percent Euro-American, 42 percent African American, 3 percent Hispanic, 1 percent Asian, and .1 percent Native American. Recent years demonstrate a clear trend of a decline in Euro-American members and an increase in all others. The challenge is to discover and affirm the common bonds that unite us as Baptists in the midst of this diversity so that it can be celebrated as part of God's creative plan.

## Peter and Paul Respond to Diversity

*Read the following stories and discuss the questions in your group.*
*Be prepared to share the results of your discussion with the class.*

### Peter and a Vision

Cornelius was a Roman centurion stationed in Caesarea, the Roman headquarters in Palestine. He had shown interest in the Jewish religion and probably had adopted many of their practices, although he had not converted to Judaism. One afternoon he had a vision in which he clearly saw an angel of God and heard the angel direct him to make contact with Peter. He immediately sent his servants in search of Peter. The next day Peter had a vision; this one was a bit more difficult to interpret. While resting on the roof of the house where he was staying, Peter saw what appeared to be a large sheet descending from heaven. In it were a variety of animals that Jews, according to their dietary laws, were not allowed to eat. A voice commanded, "Get up, Peter; kill and eat." Peter protested, knowing that it was against the Jewish law, but the voice continued until the sheet was taken back up into heaven.

From Jeffrey D. Jones, *We Are Baptists: Studies for Adults* (Valley Forge, Pa.: Judson Press, 2001).
Reproduced by permission of the publisher.

■ What do you think was the meaning of Peter's vision?

bond, faith in Christ; to embrace a new diversity of race among God's people.

■ Dietary practices were among the greatest and most divisive issues of diversity in the early church. What are the major issues of diversity today?

While Peter pondered the meaning of this vision, word came of the arrival of Cornelius's servants. After hearing their story, Peter went with them to Caesarea, where Cornelius warmly greeted him and described his vision. Peter's reply begins in Acts 10:34–35: "I now realize that it is true that God treats all men alike. Whoever fears him and does what is right is acceptable to him, no matter what race he belongs to" (TEV). The vision was a call to Peter to move beyond the common bond of the law to a new common

■ How might we apply Peter's words to today's issues?

## Paul and the Law

The churches of Galatia were in turmoil and Paul was upset. He had previously spent some time in the area and founded a number of churches. Following his departure, other itinerant preachers moved in. Among them were those who taught that gentile Christians such as the Galatians must follow the Jewish law in order to be numbered among the people of God. In response to that situation, Paul wrote a letter in which he argued strongly for a new common bond among God's people—a bond that was not law, race, social condition, or ritual practice. It was and is Christ and Christ alone.

Read Galatians 3:26–29, in which Paul's argument reached its high point, and consider the following questions.

■ Many have made the point that Paul is not speaking literally here, that differences between Jew and Greek, slave and free, male and female still obviously exist. If this is true, what is Paul's point?

■ The issue of whether Christians had to continue to observe Jewish law was one of the greatest and most divisive issues in the early church. What are the major divisive issues in the church today?

■ How might we apply Peter's words to today's issues?

## Baptist Principles

The following two principles are among those that have traditionally been affirmed as important to Baptists. Consider how each contributes to the diversity among Baptists. Then consider ways in which each helps us find a common bond that unites us.

*Soul freedom.* "The Baptist concept of soul freedom expresses the crucially important truth that all human beings can enter into direct fellowship with God, receive God's grace, and find and do God's will. When properly understood, this freedom leads not to divisive individualism or the destruction of the church or anarchy in social life. Rather, it is the assurance that God's people can form a church, build a worthwhile society, and live a Christian life under the direction of God's Spirit."[1]

*Autonomy of the local church.* "Local church autonomy means the right of each congregation (1) to choose its own ministers and officers, (2) to establish its own covenant membership and discipline and confessions, (3) to order its life in its own organizational forms with its constitution and bylaws, (4) to implement its right to belong to other denominational agencies and ecumenical bodies, (5) to own and to control its own property and budgets. . . . Our local church autonomy is constantly corrected by the lordship of Jesus Christ; by the leading of God's Spirit; by the life of the whole church, which includes all other believers whether gathered in congregational or in general church bodies; by the light of the Scriptures and the loving obedience of our personal faith and loyalty as Christians."[2]

■ In what ways do these principles explain and help Baptists deal with diversity among churches?

## Notes
1. Leland D. Hine, "Soul Freedom," *Baptist Leader,* March 1976.
2. William H. Keucher, "Congregational Autonomy," *Baptist Leader,* March 1976.

# Handout # 14

# Mission

**Biblical Basis:** Acts 1:6–11
**Key Bible Verse:** "You will be my witnesses in Jerusalem, in all Judea and Samaria, and to the ends of the earth" (Acts 1:8).

## A New Age of Mission

At one time mission was something that happened "out there"—in a place to which we sent missionaries. "Out there" might be in Africa or Asia, or any foreign land, among people who had not had the opportunity to learn about Christ. Or, it might be here in our own country among people whose physical needs were great. Most often, however, we didn't think about mission as happening in our own communities, in our own churches, through our Sunday school and our worship service.

All that has changed. Mission still happens "out there," but now it is clear that it happens, it must happen, "right here," too. We live in an unchurched society. Well over half of our fellow citizens have no significant relationship to a church. Our friends and neighbors, just as much as those halfway around the world, are in need of a Christian missionary presence in their lives so they can come to know the saving grace of Jesus Christ.

This means that our understanding of mission—where it happens, how it happens, and who does it—is expanding. Baptist national and regional mission agencies are still vitally important in the worldwide mission effort. They do things no single church could ever accomplish on its own. But now the mission work of the local congregation has taken on new meaning. Virtually every church is a mission outpost in its community, seeking to be a Christian presence in a culture and society that does not know, but needs to know, the Good News of the gospel.

Mission giving used to be something separate from the local budget of the church. Now that distinction is no longer as clear. If each church is a mission outpost, money used to support the congregation is as much mission giving as is money sent to support a missionary in another country. Both are equally important.

Mission has always been a driving force in Baptist life. Adoniram Judson, the first missionary from North America, was halfway to India before Bible study led him to a belief in believer's baptism. Baptists in the United States embraced him and his passion for mission quickly, however, once they learned they already had a Baptist missionary on the field. This same passion for mission is at work in new ways today, with a special focus on the local congregation. Baptists are a missionary people. They always have been, and by God's grace, they always will be.

From Jeffrey D. Jones, *We Are Baptists: Studies for Adults* (Valley Forge, Pa.: Judson Press, 2001). Reproduced by permission of the publisher.

# Baptist Mission Outposts

### South Providence, Rhode Island—
### A Modern Day "Judea"

South Providence has problems. They're not all that different from those found in many urban settings: poverty, poor housing, crime, an influx of immigrants who don't speak English and who find it difficult to get jobs. But good things are happening there, too—many of them the result of South Providence Neighborhood Ministries. Wanda Michaelson, the program's director, says, "On many levels our outreach to the multi-racial community in South Providence seems to be prospering: Our after-school and scouting programs are filled with happy children working on positive projects. Our English language classes are full of earnest adults struggling to comprehend the irregularities of our strange language. Our sewing class is full of adults working on clothes for themselves and their children. Our cooking and nutrition class is full of adults eager to learn new recipes and ways of making nutritious meals for their families with inexpensive ingredients." The needs are great and are responded to in a wide variety of programs—from emergency rent and utility assistance to support for those beginning small businesses, from distribution of personal care items to a program of health screenings.

In addition to these ongoing programs, Neighborhood Ministries has also organized a number of short-term activities. A "Celebrating Southside" festival with music and crafts highlighted the positive aspects of the neighborhood. During the summer, a six-week "Happy Days" program was offered for children six through twelve, which included an emphasis on multiculturalism (complete with a Chinese dragon), swimming at a state park, computer games, and special guests who taught participants about flower arranging, model trains, and playing the guitar.

South Providence Neighborhood Ministries is a mission outpost supported in part by Baptists who have a passion to be witnesses for Christ.

### The Congo—
### A Modern-Day "Samaria"

Mission in the midst of civil war and deadly epidemics—that's what it has been for Baptist missionaries in the Democratic Republic of the Congo these past few years. The civil war is over, but its effects continue to be felt. The ebola epidemic has abated, but AIDS continues its ravaging progress.

The four-hundred-bed hospital at Vanga is one of our Baptist mission outposts in the Congo. Located in a densely populated rural area in the northern part of the country, it is the only functioning healthcare facility for miles around. A place where the community is educated about healthful living and disease prevention and where healthcare workers can receive training, it is also a place where people can learn about God's love made real, both in word and deed.

The aim of the hospital and the missionaries who work in it is to meet both the physical and spiritual needs of the people. Their ministry includes education about and efforts in village sanitation, clean water, nutrition, family planning, as well as sharing the gospel and providing a setting for worship and learning about Christ. The comprehensive approach to mission that is taken here has led to the development of a great number of programs. In addition to the hospital there is a nursing school, a residency program for doctors, a fish farm, an experimental farm, a petroleum depot, a reforestation project, a village water project, a school system, and a church.

The Good News of the gospel comes in many forms in Vanga!

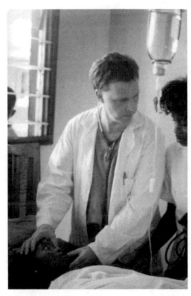

*Dr. William Clemmer at the Vanga hospital.*

# _____ Church—
# A Modern-Day "Jerusalem"

_Use the space below to describe your own church as a mission outpost._

# Baptist Heritage Resources

Brackney, William H. *Baptist Life and Thought: A Source Book*. Revised. Valley Forge, Pa.: Judson Press, 1998.

Uses primary documents from the seventeenth through the twentieth century to provide insight into important Baptist beliefs.

*Celebrate Freedom!* Macon, Ga.: Smyth and Helwys, 1998.

A Vacation Bible School curriculum based on important Baptist principles.

Gaustad, Edwin S. *Baptist Piety: The Last Will and Testimony of Obadiah Holmes*. Valley Forge, Pa.: Judson Press, 1994.

Written by a seventeenth-century Baptist leader in Rhode Island, this testimony provides revealing details about the roots, schisms, and beliefs of America's first Baptists.

Goodwin, Everett C. *Baptists in the Balance: The Tension between Freedom and Responsibility*. Valley Forge, Pa.: Judson Press, 1997.

A collection of essays, sermons, lectures, and articles that reflect a variety of perspectives on Baptist life in the late twentieth century.

Jones, Jeffrey D. *Keepers of the Faith: Illustrated Biographies from Baptist History*. Valley Forge, Pa.: Judson Press, 1999.

One-page stories of eighty important Baptists told through captioned illustrations. Can be reproduced for use as bulletin inserts or handouts.

Maring, Norman H., and Winthrop S. Hudson. *A Baptist Manual of Polity and Practice*. Revised. Valley Forge, Pa.: Judson Press, 1991.

Draws on New Testament and historical scenes to explore practical implications of the Baptist understanding of the church.

*Our American Baptist Heritage*. Video series.

A four-part video series on important events and people in American Baptist Life: The First Baptists, Baptists in Early America, Unity and Diversity in the American Baptist Movement, American Baptists Come of Age. Call 1-800-4-JUDSON to order. Valley Forge, Pa.: Board of Educational Ministries, n.d.

*People with a Mission*. Video.

A video version of a classic filmstrip that tells the story of American Baptists. Call 1-800-4-JUDSON to order. Valley Forge, Pa.: Board of Educational Ministries, n.d.

*Proclaiming the Baptist Vision*. Edited by Walter B. Shurden. Macon, Ga.: Smyth and Helwys, 1993.

Four separate volumes of sermons: *The Bible, The Church, The Priesthood of All Believers, Religious Freedom*.

Shurden, Walter B. *The Baptist Identity: Four Fragile Freedoms*. Macon, Ga.: Smyth and Helwys, 1993.

Explores historical origins and contemporary meaning of Bible, soul, religious, and church freedom. Leader's guide available.

Skodlund, John. *The Baptists*. Valley Forge, Pa.: Judson Press, 1967.

A booklet that provides a statement of commonly accepted Baptist doctrines.

Torbet, Robert G. *A History of the Baptists*. 3rd ed. Valley Forge, Pa.: Judson Press, 1963.

A classic and comprehensive history of Baptists.